Los Angeles
2008

A Selection
of **Restaurants** & **Hotels**

Let us know what you think.

Complete a brief survey at michelinguide.com/survey,
and we'll send you a promotion code good
for 20% off your next Michelin Maps & Guides
purchase at langenscheidt.com.

Receive updates, news, valuable discounts
and invitations to special events
by signing up at michelinguide.com/signup.

Offer expires 7/31/08.

Manufacture française des pneumatiques Michelin
Société en commandite par actions au capital de 304 000 000 EUR
Place des Carmes-Déchaux – 63000 Clermont-Ferrand (France)
R.C.S. Clermont-Fd B 855 200 507

No part of this publication may be reproduced in any form
without the prior permission of the publisher.

© **Michelin 2008, Propriétaires-éditeurs**
Dépot légal Novembre 2007
Printed in Canada
Published in 2007

Cover photograph : Juan Silva/Photodisc/Getty Images

Please send your comments to:

Michelin North America, Inc.
Travel Publications
One Parkway South – Greenville, SC 29615 USA
Phone: 1-800-423-0485
Fax: 1-800-378-7471
www.michelintravel.com
Michelin.guides@us.michelin.com

Dear reader

I am thrilled to launch the first edition of our Michelin Guide Los Angeles. Our teams have made every effort to produce a selection that fully reflects the rich diversity of the restaurant and hotel scene in the City of Angels.

The Michelin Guide provides a comprehensive selection and rating, in all categories of comfort and prices. As part of our meticulous and highly confidential evaluation process, Michelin's American inspectors conducted anonymous visits to restaurants and hotels in Los Angeles. Michelin's inspectors are the eyes and ears of the customers, and thus their anonymity is key to ensure that they receive the same treatment as any other guest. The decision to award a star is a collective one, based on the consensus of all inspectors who have visited a particular establishment.

Our company's two founders, Édouard and André Michelin, published the first Michelin Guide in 1900, to provide motorists with practical information about where they could service and repair their cars, and find quality accommodations and a good meal. The star-rating system for outstanding restaurants was introduced in 1926. The same system is used for our American selections.

I sincerely hope that the Michelin Guide Los Angeles 2008 will become your favorite guide to the city's restaurants and hotels. On behalf of all our Michelin employees, let me wish you the very best enjoyment in your Los Angeles dining and hotel experiences.

Michel Rollier
Chief Executive Officer, Michelin

Contents

BEVERLY HILLS   34

▶ Bel-Air

GREATER DOWNTOWN   58

▶ Chinatown
▶ Koreatown

HOLLYWOOD   70

▶ Midtown
▶ West Hollywood

PASADENA 110

SANTA MONICA BAY 122

▶ Malibu
▶ Marina del Rey
▶ Venice

VENTURA BOULEVARD 150

▶ Agoura Hills
▶ Calabasas
▶ Westlake Village

WESTSIDE 164

▶ Brentwood
▶ Century City
▶ Culver City
▶ West LA
▶ Westwood

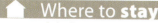

Where to **stay**

How to use this guide

Hotels classified according to comfort
(more pleasant if in red)

🏠 Quite comfortable

🏠🏠 Comfortable

🏠🏠🏠 Very comfortable

🏠🏠🏠 Top class comfort

🏠🏠🏠🏠 Luxury in the traditional style

Map References
(Hotels)

Average Prices
Prices do not include applicable taxes

Price classification
(Hotels)
$ under $150
$$ $150 to $250
$$$ $250 to $350
$$$$ over $350

Hotel symbols
149 rooms No. of rooms and suites
🚪 Wheelchair access
ᓮ Exercise room
⚙ Spa
🏊 Swimming pool
🏛 Equipped conference room

Star for good food
❀ to ❀❀❀

Restaurant symbols
🍽 Cash only
🚪 Wheelchair access
🌿 Garden or terrace dining
🍽 Brunch
🍷 A particularly interesting wine list
👔 Jacket required
🅿 Valet parking
🕯 Late dining

Los Angeles areas or neighborhoods
Each area is color coded...
■ Beverly Hills
■ Greater Downtown
■ Hollywood
■ Pasadena
■ Santa Monica Bay
■ Ventura Boulevard
■ Westside

The Hotel

🏠🏠🏠

001
359 Green St. (at Oak Ave.)
Phone: 213-234-5555 or 800-123-4567
Fax: 213-234-5555
Web: www.thehotel.com
Prices: $$$$

200 Rooms
23 Suites
🚪
ᓮ
🏊

Italian Restaurant ❀❀❀

Italian 🍴🍴

002
111 Santa Monica Blvd. (at Wilshire Blvd.)
Phone: 310-456-7777   Mon - Fri lunch & dinner
Web: www.ItalianRestaurant.com   Sat - Sun dinner only
Prices: $$$

Beverly Hills

Pasadena

🚪
🍽
🌿
🍷
🕯

Step into the Italian Restaurant and feel like you have taken a trip to Italy without ever leaving the city. It's no wonder that this restaurant, with its main dining room lighted with 750 custom candles, and set with Limoges china and Baroque-style furnishings, is prized for an enchanting evening out.
In this sanctuary of classic Italian cuisine, you can choose your own dishes within the framework of a three-, four-, or five-course prix-fixe menu. Although it constantly changes, the selection includes a long list of Italian favorites (Spaghetti Bolognese, White Pizza and Gnocchi), many interpreted with local products. For non-meat eaters, a vegetarian tasting menu is always an option.
On the wine list, you'll discover an excellent selection of Italian varietals, including Chianti from the chef's native Puglia region.

Appetizers	Entrées	Desserts
• Seafood Salad	• Hamburger with Blue Cheese	• Crème Brûlée
• Spicy Shrimp	• Macaroni and Cheese	• Tiramisu
• Seared Tuna	• Grilled Chicken in a Peach Sauce	• Coconut Cake

100

Restaurants classified according to comfort (more pleasant if in red)	✗ Quite comfortable	✗✗ Very comfortable	✗✗✗ Top class comfort	✗✗✗✗✗ Luxury in the traditional style
	✗✗ Comfortable			

Name, address and information about the establishment

Map References (Restaurants)

Price classification (Restaurants)

⌾	under $25
$$	$25 to $40
$$$	$40 to $60
$$$$	over $60

Antica Osteria

001

Italian ✗✗

223 Hollywood Blvd. (N. Orange Dr.)

Phone: 213-444-5555
Web: www.anticaosteria.com
Prices: $$$

Mon – Fri lunch & dinner
Sat – Sun dinner only

Hollywood

Meat lovers, rejoice! The Brazilian concept at this restaurant means that for one set price, you can eat all you want. A variety of meats (pork loin, ribs, top sirloin of beef, sausage, chicken) is cooked on skewers over an open fire and brought straight to your table by a waiter clad in gaucho garb. They'll keep bringing food until you tell them to stop or when they run out of food. A neon sign placed on your table will inform the staff of the state of your appetite: flip the green switch for 'go' or the red switch for 'stop'.

To go with all that tasty meat, there's a salad bar, a buffet of side dishes, and your choice of dessert. Wine racks and Brazilian landscape paintings embellish the colorful dining space.

Perch ✿✿

001

Seafood ✗✗✗✗

300 Sunset Blvd. (at Crescent Dr.)

Phone: 310-234-5555
Web: www.perch.us
Prices: $$$$

Mon - Fri lunch & dinner
Sat - Sun dinner only

Beverly Hills

American ✗✗

t Sixth Ave.)

Lunch & dinner daily

oice! This Mediterranean meze house
ual, convivial atmosphere. A variety of
quash, tomatoes, mushrooms) is cooked
r an open fire and brought straight to your
ter clad in overalls. Homemade yogurt
r and garlic is served along with your
he recipes come from Turkey, but there
ebanese items as well.

all of the tasty tofu, jump in line for the all-
at of wine. After your meal, treat yourself
us chocolate pie.

100

The city's special-occasion spot for more than 40 years, the restaurant now operates under the auspices of chef and owner Bill Smith. It's no wonder that his restaurant, with its romantic main dining room lighted with 900 custom candles, and set with Limoges china and Louis XVI-style furnishings, is prized for an enchanting evening out.

In this sanctuary of classic French cuisine, you can choose your own dishes within the framework of a three-, four-, or five-course prix-fixe menu. Although it constantly changes, the selection includes a long list of French favorites (peppered filet mignon with braised endive, boneless quail stuffed with ris de veau, Grand Marnier soufflé), many interpreted with California products. For non-meat eaters, a vegetarian tasting menu is always an option.

On the wine list, you'll discover an excellent selection of French varietals, including Riesling from the chef's native Alsace region, as well as white Burgundy and red Bordeaux.

Appetizers	Entrées	Desserts
• Ahi Tuna Tartare	• Peppered Filet Mignon	• Chocolate Composition
• Trio of Cold Artisan Foie Gras	• Grand Marnier Soufflé	• Coffee Mousse Bar
• Sesame-crusted Hamachi, Yuru Shiso, Shiitake Mushroom Salad	• Boneless Quail stuffed with Ris de Veau	• Coconut Soufflé

Sample menu for starred restaurants

101

How to use this guide

7

A brief history of Los Angeles

The four million people who live inside LA's 469 square miles speak more than 90 languages in a mosaic of communities comprising the nation's most multicultural city—a literal and figurative melting pot that boasts a nearly year-round growing season as well as some 15,000 restaurants.

PROVINCIAL NO MORE

Our Lady the Queen of the Angels was founded in 1781 by 11 families who answered the call of Felipe de Neve (the Spanish governor of California) for *pobladores*, or settlers, for a new town in southern California. Food was a priority here from the beginning. The settlement's 44 pioneers were charged with feeding the garrison guarding the pueblo. Grains and game were staples until land-grant ranchers began to produce beef for local tables.

Mexico's independence from Spain in 1821 opened the province to non-Spanish immigrants. In the 1830s, French Angelenos planted the pueblo's first orange grove and California's first vineyards. Ceded to the U.S. in 1848, California soon swarmed with Gold Rush fortune-seekers who brought seeds from afar, sprouting the region's diverse agriculture. In the 1850s, as hunters supplied restaurants with bear meat, émigrés from Italy's high regions were winning tastes away from mining-camp fare in favor of the Northern Italian recipes that still pepper area menus.

Chinese recruited to build the western leg of the

©Mark Gibson

©Mark Gibson

Transcontinental Railroad later established California's fishing industry, selling catches along the Los Angeles shore. In 1885 the city's first Japanese-owned venture, a restaurant, marked the birth of Little Tokyo.

INNOVATION LEADS TO FUSION

Local oil booms in the 1890s and the early 20th-century arrival of movie companies created a free-spending elite associated with nightclubbing and fancy dining, barely constrained by Prohibition or the Depression that followed. A 1905 Los Angeles Times cookbook hints of things to come: a "California Salad" calling for walnuts and the "purest olive oil." Still, through the Eisenhower years, the city remained, as one newspaperman observed, "a red meat, red sauce, heavy cream and butter town."

That changed in the 1960s, as jet planes delivered fresh foods from around the globe and local farmers'

markets proliferated. Waves of immigration from Latin America, Asia, Iran, Africa and the former Soviet Bloc established vibrant ethnic communities, each a constituency for homeland cuisines. The professional stigma associated with their inevitable Americanization began to fade after a chef at one of LA's first sushi bars, unable to find fresh toro, substituted creamy avocado for the fatty tuna belly. The California roll's immediate popularity opened the door to cross-culinary combinations. This dynamic approach was pursued most famously by Austrian-born chef Wolfgang Puck, whose bold experiments, like blending French techniques with Asian ingredients, came to be called fusion cooking. The result is a unique, ever-evolving local cuisine, the best of it fresh, organic, locally produced and seasonal.

Note that valet parking is available at most restaurants in LA.

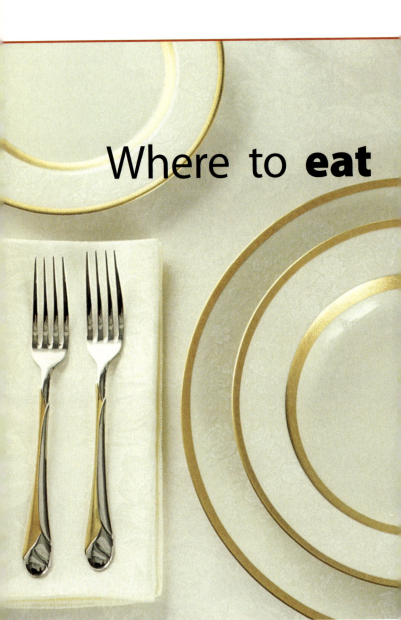

Where to **eat**

Alphabetical list of Restaurants

A

A.O.C.	✗✗	73
Abode	✗✗	124
Akwa	✗✗	124
Alcove	✗	73
All' Angelo	✗✗	74
Amici	✗✗	125
Angelini Osteria	✗	74
Angolo DiVino	✗✗	166
Arroyo Chop House	✗✗	112
Asakuma	✗✗	166
Asanebo	✿ ✗	152
Asia de Cuba	✗✗	75
Axe	✗	125

B

Banzai Sushi	✗	153
Baran	✗✗✗	167
Barefoot	✗	75
Bar Marmont	✗	76
Beacon	✗	167
Belvedere (The)	✗✗✗	36
BIN 8945	✗	76
Bistro 45	✗✗	112
Bistro 561	✗✗	113
Blair's	✗✗	77
BLD	✗✗	77
Blue Velvet	✗✗	60
Blvd (The)	✗✗✗	36
BOA	✗✗	78
Bombay Café	✗✗	168
Border Grill	✗✗	126
Boss Sushi	✗	37
Brandywine	✗✗	153
Breeze	✗✗	168
Brentwood Restaurant & Lounge	✗✗	169
Buffalo Club (The)	✗✗✗	126

C

Cafe del Rey	✗✗	127
Café 14	✗✗	154
Café des Artistes	✗	78
Cafe Pinot	✗✗	60
Caffe Delfini	✗✗	127
Campanile	✗✗✗	79
Capo	✗✗	128
Carlitos Gardel	✗✗	79
Catch	✗✗	128
Celadon	✗✗	80
Celestino	✗✗	113
Chabuya	✗	169
Chakra	✗✗✗	37
Chameau	✗✗	80
Chaya Brasserie	✗✗	81
Chaya Venice	✗✗	129
Checkers Downtown	✗✗✗	61
Chinois on Main	✗	129
Cholada	✗	130
Cicada	✗✗✗	61
Clay Pit (The)	✗✗	170
Crustacean	✗✗✗	38
CUT	✿ ✗✗✗	39

D

Dakota	✗✗✗	81
Danube	✗	170
Darya	✗✗	171
Da Vinci	✗✗✗	38
Derek's	✗✗✗	114
Dining Room at the Ritz-Carlton, Huntington (The) ✿	✗✗✗✗	115
Divino	✗✗	171
Dolce Enoteca	✗✗	82
Doug Arango's	✗✗	82
Drago	✗✗✗	130
Dusty's	✗	83

E

E. Baldi	✗✗	40
eat. on sunset	✗✗	83

Mélisse	✿✿ XxX	138
Michael's	XX	137
Mimosa	X	96
Mirabelle	XX	96
Mirü8691	XX	46
Monte Alban	XX	180
Moonshadows	X	139
Mori Sushi	✿ X	181
Mr Chow	XX	48

N

Nanbankan	X	180
Napa Valley Grille	XX	182
Native Foods	X	182
Nick & Stef's Steakhouse	XX	63
Nic's	XX	48
Nishimura	X	97
Nizam of India	XX	183
Nobu	X	139
Noé	XxX	64
Nook Bistro	XX	183
Nyala Ethiopian	X	97

O

Ocean Avenue Seafood	XX	140
Off Vine	XX	98
One Pico	XxX	140
Onyx	XX	158
Orris	XX	184
Ortolan	✿ XxX	99
Osteria Latini	XX	184

P

Palmeri Ristorante	XX	185
Panzanella	XX	158
Park's Barbeque	X	64
Parkway Grill	XxX	116
Pastis	X	98
Patina	✿ XxXX	65
Pecorino	XX	185
Penthouse (The)	XX	141
Piccolo	XX	141
Piccolo Paradiso	XX	49
Pinot Bistro	XX	159
Pizzeria Mozza	X	100
Pizzicotto	X	186

Polo Lounge	XxX	49
Porta Via	X	50
Prime Grill (The)	XxX	50
Primitivo Wine Bistro	XX	142
Providence	✿ XxX	101

R

Raymond (The)	XX	117
Real Food Daily	X	142
Republic	XX	100
Restaurant at Hotel Bel-Air (The)	XxX	51
Restaurant at the Getty Center	XxX	186
Riviera	XxX	159
Royale	XX	66
R 23	XX	66
Rustic Canyon	XX	143

S

Saddle Peak Lodge	✿ XxX	160
Saketini	X	187
Saladang Song	X	117
Sam's by the Beach	XX	143
Sapori	XX	144
750 ml	XX	118
Shaherzad	X	187
Shima	XX	144
Shiro	XX	118
SIMON L.A.	XX	102
Social Hollywood	XxX	102
Sona	✿ XxXX	103
Sonora Café	XX	104
Spago	✿✿ XxX	52
Stinking Rose (The)	X	51
Suki 7	XX	161
Surya	X	104
Sushi & Kushi Imai	X	53
Sushi Dokoro Ki Ra La	X	53
Sushi House Unico	XX	54
Sushi Iki	X	161
Sushi Nozawa	X	162
Sushi Roku	XX	105
Sushi Sasabune	X	188
Sushi Sushi	X	54
Sushi Yotsuya	X	162

Restaurants by Cuisine Type

American

Alcove	73
BLD	77
Blvd (The)	36
Brentwood Restaurant & Lounge	169
Buffalo Club (The)	126
Dakota	81
Doug Arango's	82
Grill on the Alley (The)	42
Josie	132
Michael's	137
Moonshadows	139
Saddle Peak Lodge	160
Vibrato	55

Argentinian

Carlitos Gardel	79

Asian

Beacon	167
Chinois on Main	129
Crustacean	38
Mako	45
Mirü8691	46
Saketini	187
Typhoon	146
Zip Fusion	192

Bakery

3 Square Café & Bakery	145

Bulgarian

Danube	170

Californian

Axe	125
Barefoot	75
Bistro 45	112
Bistro 561	113
Blair's	77
Breeze	168
Café 14	154
Checkers Downtown	61
Derek's	114
Hampton's	155
Hatfield's	86
JiRaffe	132
J Lounge	63
Joe's	133
Literati II	179
M Café de Chaya	95
Mirabelle	96
Napa Valley Grille	182
Off Vine	98
One Pico	140
Parkway Grill	116
Polo Lounge	49
Porta Via	50
Raymond (The)	117
Restaurant at the Getty Center	186
Rustic Canyon	143
Spago	52
Table 8	105
Tower Bar	107
208 Rodeo	55
Violet	148
Whist	149
Wilshire	149
Yabu	109

Chinese

Empress Pavilion	62
Mr Chow	48
Yang Chow	67
Yujean Kang's	120

Contemporary

Abode	124
Bar Marmont	76
Belvedere (The)	36
BIN 8945	76

Japanese

Korean

Latin American

Mediterranean

Mexican

Moroccan

Persian

Seafood

Southwestern

Steakhouse

Thai

Vegan

Where to eat ▶ Restaurants by Cuisine Type

Cuisine Type by area

BEVERLY HILLS

American
Blvd (The)	✕✕✕	36
Grill on the Alley (The)	✕✕	42
Vibrato	✕✕	55

Asian
Crustacean	✕✕✕	38
Mako	✕✕	45
Mirü8691	✕✕	46

Californian
Polo Lounge	✕✕✕	49
Porta Via	✕	50
Spago	❀❀ ✕✕✕	52
208 Rodeo	✕✕	55

Chinese
Mr Chow	✕✕	48

Contemporary
Belvedere (The)	✕✕✕	36
Gardens	✕✕✕	41

French
Restaurant at Hotel Bel-Air (The)	✕✕✕	51

Indian
Chakra	✕✕✕	37

International
Nic's	✕✕	48

Italian
Da Vinci	✕✕✕	38
E. Baldi	✕✕	40
Enoteca Drago	✕✕	40
Il Buco	✕✕	43
Il Cielo	✕✕	44
Il Pastaio	✕	44
Massimo	✕✕	45
Piccolo Paradiso	✕✕	49
Stinking Rose (The)	✕	51

Japanese
Boss Sushi	✕	37
Gonpachi	✕✕✕	42
Hokusai	✕✕	43
Matsuhisa	❀ ✕	47
Sushi & Kushi Imai	✕	53
Sushi Dokoro Ki Ra La	✕	53
Sushi House Unico	✕✕	54
Sushi Sushi	✕	54
Urasawa	❀❀ ✕✕	56

Mexican
Frida	✕✕	41

Steakhouse
CUT	❀ ✕✕✕	39
Mastro's	✕✕✕	46
Prime Grill (The)	✕✕✕	50

GREATER DOWNTOWN

Californian
Checkers Downtown	✕✕✕	61
J Lounge	✕✕	63

Chinese
Empress Pavilion	✕	62
Yang Chow	✕	67

Contemporary
Blue Velvet	✕✕	60
Cafe Pinot	✕✕	60
Cicada	✕✕✕	61
Noé	✕✕✕	64
Patina	❀ ✕✕✕✕	65
Royale	✕✕	66

Japanese
Izayoi	✕	62
R 23	✕✕	66
Thousand Cranes	✕✕	67

Korean
Park's Barbeque	✕	64
Yong Su San	✕✕	69

Seafood
Water Grill	❀ ✕✕✕	68

Steakhouse
Nick & Stef's Steakhouse	✕✕	63

HOLLYWOOD

American
Alcove	✕	73

Where to eat ▶ Cuisine Type by area

23

Live in Italian

Starred Restaurants

*W*ithin the selection we offer you, some restaurants deserve to be highlighted for their particularly good cuisine. When giving one, two or three Michelin stars, there are a number of things that we judge, including the quality of the ingredients, the technical skill and flair that goes into their preparation, the blend and clarity of flavors, and the balance of the menu. Just as important is the ability to produce excellent cooking time and again. We make as many visits as we need, so that our readers can be sure of quality and consistency.

A two- or three-star restaurant has to offer something very special in its cuisine; a real element of creativity, originality or "personality" that sets it apart from the rest. Three stars —our highest award—are given to the very best restaurants, where the whole dining experience is superb.

Cuisine in any style, modern or traditional, may be eligible for a star. Because we apply the same independent standards everywhere, the awards have become benchmarks of reliability and excellence in more than 20 European countries, particularly in France, where we have awarded stars for almost 80 years, and where the expression "Now that's real three-star quality!" has entered into the language.

The awarding of a star is based solely on the quality of the cuisine.

✿✿✿

Exceptional cuisine, worth a special journey.

One always eats here extremely well, sometimes superbly.
Distinctive dishes are precisely executed, using superlative
ingredients.

✿✿

Excellent cuisine, worth a detour.

Skillfully and carefully crafted dishes of outstanding quality.

Mélisse	✗✗✗	138
Spago	✗✗✗	52
Urasawa	✗✗	56

✿

A very good restaurant in its category.

A place offering cuisine prepared to a consistently high
standard.

Asanebo	✗	152
CUT	✗✗✗	39
Dining Room at the Ritz-Carlton, Huntington (The)	✗✗✗✗	115
Joe's	✗✗	133
La Botte	✗✗	134
Matsuhisa	✗	47
Mori Sushi	✗	181
Ortolan	✗✗✗	99
Patina	✗✗✗✗	65
Providence	✗✗✗	101
Saddle Peak Lodge	✗✗✗	160
Sona	✗✗✗✗	103
Trattoria Tre Venezie	✗✗	119
Valentino	✗✗✗	147
Water Grill	✗✗✗	68

Where to **eat** ▶ Starred Restaurants

Where to eat for less than $25

FINE DINING WATER FROM TUSCANY

Where to have brunch

Where to eat ▶ Where to have brunch

Where to have a late dinner

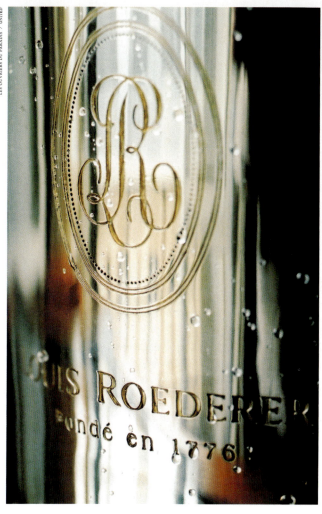

LOUIS ROEDERER

CHAMPAGNE

Beverly Hills

Bel-Air

Between West Hollywood and West Los Angeles, roughly bounded on the south by Whitworth Drive, this palmy city of 36,000 inclines north along curving streets, crossing Sunset Boulevard into the Santa Monica Mountains where its grandest homes rise behind tall hedges and gates.

Nine-tenths of Beverly Hills' 5.7 square miles are residential, so the city's stellar shopping and dining cluster around **Rodeo Drive** in the pedestrian-friendly **Golden Triangle** bound by Santa Monica Boulevard, Wilshire Boulevard and Rexford Drive. Though most residents are professional and business people, the city remains the perceived capital of A-list extravagance, displayed by a conspicuous minority addicted to pampering, cosmetic surgery and the costliest of everything.

FROM SWALE TO SWANK

The confluence of streams from Franklin, Coldwater and Benedict canyons led the native Gabrielino-Tongva people to name the area The Gathering of the Waters. In 1838 a land grant to Maria Rita Valdez Villa, the Afro-Latina widow of a Spanish soldier, bestowed the parcel called El Rodeo de las Aguas. Employing a corps of *vaqueros* out of her adobe near Sunset Boulevard and Alpine Drive, she raised cattle and horses until 1854, selling her 4,449-acre rancho—more than a square

mile larger than present-day Beverly Hills—for $4,000.

The late 1800s brought a run of failed oil and building schemes, the last a North African-themed subdivision called Morocco. In 1907 developers filed papers for "Beverly Hills" (the name reflects a partner's fondness for Beverly Farms, Massachusetts), its big lots and high prices targeting the wealthy. In 1912 the Beverly Hills Hotel became the community's social center. Among filmdom's first millionaires were Mary Pickford and her husband, Douglas Fairbanks, whose 1919 move into their Summit Drive estate, Pickfair, triggered an influx of screen stars.

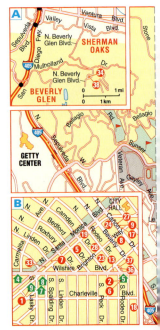

Located less than a mile up Beverly Boulevard from Sunset, Coldwater Canyon Park offers serenity amid the buzz, as do the terraced gardens of the Doheny oil clan's 1928 Greystone estate that overlooks the city. On Sunday mornings, just east of City Hall on Civic Center Drive, the **Beverly Hills Farmers' Market** recalls this area's cultivation by 19th-century vegetable peddlers.

Bel-Air

Laid out in 1923 behind imposing white gates north of Sunset, this woodsy enclave (a part of Los Angeles) climbs the ridges above Beverly Hills. This area is a bastion of privacy, most of its posh residences hidden by greenery. Even its unofficial clubhouse, the Hotel Bel-Air, is easy to miss as you drive by.

©Mark Gibson

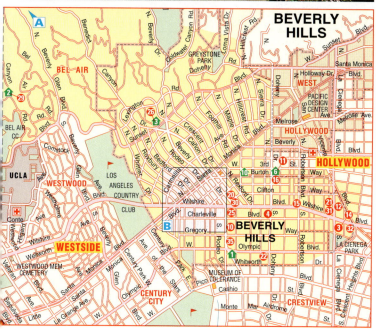

The Belvedere

001

Contemporary ✗✗✗

9882 South Santa Monica Blvd. (at Wilshire Blvd.)

Phone:	310-788-2306
Web:	www.beverlyhills.peninsula.com
Prices:	$$$$

Lunch & dinner daily

Money's in the air in the classy Peninsula Beverly Hills *(see hotel listing)*. The Belvedere's high-bourgeois décor—the gilt-framed paintings, three-tiered table linens, French antiques—along with the cool reserve of the restaurant's knowledgeable sommelier, would make a doyen of the Seventh Arrondissement feel right at home. Yet the nervous efficiency seems more like Beverly Hills upscale than Parisian upper class.

The ambition is here, in the likes of California foie gras with rhubarb and vanilla, and dry-aged signature meats. The look is here, too, but attention to culinary detail can fall short of continental standards. Even so, such a service-oriented establishment, where support staff move at a rifleman's trot, may yet find its way.

The Blvd

002

American ✗✗✗

9500 Wilshire Blvd. (at Rodeo Dr.)

Phone:	310-275-5200
Web:	www.fourseasons.com/beverlywilshire
Prices:	$$$$

Lunch & dinner daily

In the Beverly Wilshire hotel *(see hotel listing)* facing Wilshire at Rodeo Drive, this grand room enjoys one of the city's top locations, a reason the sidewalk tables are so highly coveted. High ceilings, panelled walls, graceful armchairs and finely set wood tables strike a refined tone for hotel guests and locals, including the occasional famous face.

Prepared with skill and superb ingredients, globally influenced cuisine trumps star-gazing. An Ahi tuna sampler presents seared slices of fish atop a julienne of green papaya, as well as a stack of diced avocado crowned with Ahi tartare. The all-day schedule allows the prime sirloin Blvd Burger, with foie gras mousse and sautéed wild mushrooms, to fit right in.

Dress to impress—it matters here.

Boss Sushi

J a p a n e s e ✗

270A S. La Cienega Blvd. (at Wilshire Blvd.)

Phone:	310-659-5612	Mon – Sat lunch & dinner
Web:	www.bosssushi.com	Sun dinner only
Prices:	⊖⊖	

♿ "A modern collision of east and west" is how Tom "The Boss" Sagara describes the exuberant pairing of his own sauces with traditional sushi and sashimi combinations. His spacious workplace includes a long sushi bar. Casual furnishings, random colors and an abundance of car-racing photos and memorabilia reflect Sagara's determination to stay at the front of the pack. (Like the drivers racing across the walls of Boss Sushi, LA's sushi chefs are competitive and keenly aware of their rivals.) Sagara's forte is flavorful sushi rolls—how about minced raw tuna seasoned with red chile, sliced green scallions and sesame oil, wrapped in nori? His expertly simple presentations honor the art, at low prices rarely found in Beverly Hills.

Chakra

I n d i a n ✗✗✗

151 S. Doheny Dr. (at Charleville Blvd.)

Phone:	310-246-3999	Lunch & dinner daily
Web:	www.chakracuisine.com	
Prices:	**$$**	

Sheer veils, earth tones and votive candles soften the modern lines of this spacious hideaway, whose patio tables are sheltered from street bustle by greenery.
Appetizers transform familiar ingredients into unusual delectables like mixed-vegetable patties served with mint and tamarind sauce, and tandoori-cooked mushrooms stuffed with cheese. If chutneys are offered with a crispy *pappadam* (a thin round wafer made, in this case, with chickpea flour), say yes. Chicken, lamb and shrimp are featured traditional entrées, but look for specials like the Punjabi favorite *channa masala*—chickpeas stewed in a brown sauce edgy with ginger, toasted cumin, spices, sliced red onions and cilantro. These may be foods of humble origin, but this is fine dining.

Crustacean

Asian

005

9646 South Santa Monica Blvd. (at Bedford Dr.)

Phone: 310-205-8990
Web: www.anfamily.com
Prices: **$$$**

Mon – Fri lunch & dinner
Sat – Sun dinner only

Industry players, whose lust for privilege is second only to breathing, buzz over this Euro-Vietnamese extravaganza's "secret" family kitchen. Inside, a glass walkway spans a koi pond and leads to a paneled, two-story dining room inspired by the An family's former French Colonial estate in Hanoi.

Garlic noodles (with a "secret sauce") are much ordered, though most ingredients are pleasingly evident. "Asian Tapas" starters include tasty rice-paper rolls full of crisp vegetables and sweet prawns. Salads, near-entrées in themselves, are liberally tossed with scallops, prawns, salmon, calamari or beef. "Large Plates" of fish, chicken and lamb encourage sharing.

The downside? The crush of diners in this popular place may hamper service.

Da Vinci

Italian

007

9737 South Santa Monica Blvd. (at Linden Dr.)

Phone: 310-273-0960
Web: www.davincibeverlyhills.com
Prices: **$$$**

Mon – Fri lunch & dinner
Sat – Sun dinner only

His standing order on arrival was two Cutty Sarks, and Dean Martin claimed them often, slipping into his reserved booth in this ornately mirrored place he proclaimed his favorite. Tuxedoed servers may finish dishes tableside, but their easy, friendly manner bans stiffness from the hushed and intimate room, which, besides crooners, attracts an old-school Beverly Hills crowd as well.

The menu presents Italian classics, starting with generous appetizers like prosciutto-wrapped grilled asparagus. A signature dish, *Pollo Da Vinci*, combines thinly pounded chicken breast with rounds of fennel-seed-scented Italian sausage, strips of roasted bell pepper and sliced roasted white mushrooms. For dessert, try the tiramisú; it's one of the best in town.

CUT ❀

9500 Wilshire Blvd. (at Rodeo Dr.)

Phone:	310-276-8500	Mon – Sat dinner only
Web:	www.wolfgangpuck.com	
Prices:	$$$$	

Beverly Hills

Timothy Griffith/Four Seasons

Cuisine by Wolfgang Puck, design by Richard Meier… the whole *très chic* shebang ensconced inside the opulent Beverly Wilshire *(see hotel listing)*. Attentive waiters, abstract paintings hung in an immaculate, airy space of blond wood floors, bare wood tables and comfy leather banquettes make CUT as thoroughly Beverly Hills as the Aston-Martins and Bentleys dropping actors and producers at the parking stands outside.

Puck successfully redefines his chosen genre, here the American steakhouse. Meats including Wagyu beef—the real thing, imported from Japan—are grilled then briefly broiled at 1,200 degrees, creating a smoky, charred crust that seals in the juices. Sumptuous side dishes run to treats like organic asparagus with poached egg and warm bacon vinaigrette.

To make the cut: don't expect to walk in and get a table; don't try to find your own parking; dress up.

Appetizers	*Entrées*	*Desserts*
• Prime Sirloin Steak Tartare, Herb Aïoli	• Indian Spiced, Slowly Cooked Short Ribs	• Baby Banana Cream Pie Brûlée, Dark Chocolate Sorbet
• Bone Marrow Flan, Mushroom Marmalade, Parsley Salad	• Grilled U.S.D.A. Prime Beef, Nebraska Corn Fed, Dry Aged 35 Days	• Valrhona Chocolate Soufflé, Milk Chocolate Hazelnut Glacé
• Maryland Blue Crab and Louisiana Shrimp "Louis" Cocktail	• Roasted Maine Lobster, Truffle Sabayon	• Wild Berry Crumble, Vanilla Ice Cream

E. Baldi

Italian ✗✗

375 N. Cañon Dr. (at Brighton Way)

Phone:	310-248-2633	Mon – Sat lunch & dinner
Web:	www.ebaldi.com	
Prices:	**$$$$**	

The Baldi family's reputation is anchored by Giorgio Baldi's eponymous Santa Monica bistro. Run by Giorgio's son, Eduardo, sibling E. Baldi sits on a busy Beverly Hills shopping street. It has a more modern look but draws the same upscale crowd for lunch and dinner.

Using fine ingredients, dishes are expertly prepared to preserve natural flavors. An heirloom tomato and buffalo mozzarella salad is drizzled with fragrant olive oil and sprinkled with fresh basil. Italian sea bass and fresh langoustines are roasted, simply topped with a sprinkle of lemon juice and olive oil, and served with roasted artichoke hearts. Desserts like chocolate crêpes folded over a hazelnut mousse define the craft.

Looks like the new kid on the block has a bright future.

Enoteca Drago

Italian ✗✗

410 N. Cañon Dr. (at Brighton Way)

Phone:	310-786-8236	Lunch & dinner daily
Web:	www.celestinodrago.com	
Prices:	**$$**	

There's an authentic feeling to this pleasant bistro, whose name *(enoteca)* means wine cellar. Celestino Drago wanted to create a "quintessential neighborhood *ristorante*, wine bar and pizzeria." He has, offering a good selection of wines by the glass and familiar fare with confident touches, like penne with prosciutto and vodka sauce, or beef filet carpaccio with raw baby artichokes and thin slices of aged Parmagiano Reggiano.

Italians expect their neighborhood restaurant to fill them up, despite the enoteca tradition of small plates. Drago does. No need to hunt for the clams in the *linguine alle vongole veraci*, fragrant with olive oil and garlic; there are plenty.

When the weather's comfortable, the outside terrace makes an appealing roost.

Frida

010

Mexican

236 S. Beverly Dr. (bet. Charleville Blvd. & Gregory Way)

Phone:	310-278-7666	Tue – Sat lunch & dinner
Web:	www.fridarestaurant.com	Sun – Mon dinner only
Prices:	$$	

Everyone knows which Frida we mean, so it's no surprise the interior is artistically cluttered and colorful, sophisticated and rustic by turns. Stone tile floors, bright walls, a big canvas of rural life, wrought-iron fixtures and woven reed chairs create a perfect setting for gourmet food true to Mexican tradition.

You see it even in the crispy corn chips and the salsas, which mix the freshest vegetables, herbs and spices; and the guacamole, one version roused with raw white onion, spicy Serrano chile and fresh cilantro.

Like Frida Kahlo, the main courses are seductively complicated. A chicken breast comes covered in a rich, nutty and delicious ground-pumpkin-seed mole, flanked by black beans and stock-flavored rice, with a cornmeal fritter. Brava!

Gardens

011

Contemporary

300 S. Doheny Dr. (at Burton Way)

Phone:	310-273-2222	Lunch & dinner daily
Web:	www.fourseasons.com	
Prices:	$$$$	

Surrounded by palms and lush foliage, Gardens' dining room nestles off the lobby of the Four Seasons Beverly Hills *(see hotel listing)*, where it creates a sense of seclusion and luxury befitting its swanky hotel home.

Each course unfolds with flavors that are at once intricate and balanced. Good ingredients and artful presentation are evident in dishes such as a fillet of roasted black cod marinated in citrus-sesame dressing and served atop a cylinder of green basmati rice and wilted chard. For the finale, the pastry chef may whip up a flourless chocolate cake with vanilla-bean ice cream.

Well-versed servers proffer an efficiency that marries well with the dining room's 18th-century French style and the casual elegance of the adjoining terrace.

Gonpachi

Japanese ✗✗✗

012

134 N. La Cienega Blvd. (bet. Clifton Way & Wilshire Blvd.)

Phone:	310-659-8887
Web:	N/A
Prices:	**$$$**

Dinner daily

Through a raked garden over a trickling stream, the path to Gonpachi leads to a re-creation of a Japanese estate house. Filled with artifacts and details like sliding *shoji* doors and carved railings, it fosters the tranquility associated with these sanctuaries. Handmade wood tables overlook sushi and charcoal-fired *sumiyaki* areas. Private rooms and *tatami* alcoves accommodate guests, sans shoes, who sit on woven mats.

Sushi, sashimi and cooked entrées, including meats grilled on bamboo skewers, fill the menu. Gonpachi's homemade buckwheat soba noodles are so flavorful they may be served simply with a bit of wasabi and a soy dipping sauce. Beverages include a good selection of sake and *shochu*, a distilled drink similar to vodka.

The Grill on the Alley

American ✗✗

013

9560 Dayton Way (at Wilshire Blvd.)

Phone:	310-276-0615
Web:	www.thegrill.com
Prices:	**$$$**

Mon – Sat lunch & dinner
Sun dinner only

The interior evokes the confident era when Ike was president, cars with pistons the size of paint cans burned 25-cent-per-gallon gasoline, and day's end meant a martini (mixed here in many varieties) or a scotch. It's all present and accounted for: comfy booths, ceiling molding, a big mirror reflecting an affluent patronage and a staff focused on service, not the next audition.

Appetizers are a traditional glossary: shrimp cocktail, oysters on the half shell, with sashimi perhaps thrown in for local color. Sides and salads are many and nostalgically familiar, from a big Caesar to a bowl of creamed spinach. The flag flies over steaks and chops—that's what you salute here, aged prime Angus Midwestern corn-fed beef, succulent pork and veal.

Hokusai

014

Japanese ✗✗

8400 Wilshire Blvd. (at Gale Dr.)

Phone: 323-782-9718
Web: www.hokusairestaurant.com
Prices: $$$

Mon – Fri lunch & dinner
Sat dinner only

High ceilings, dark wood floors and walls, white linen and creamy leather alcove banquettes evoke the soaring sets seen in musicals once made in this town, which drew everyone's eyes up along with their spirits.

If you don't have a dance partner, the dining bar offers solo seating and camaraderie with the open kitchen staff. Plates beg to be shared—lightly pickled vegetable appetizers tossed in oil, seasoned with salt and chopped jalapeño. Nothing generic here: a wedge of steamed *bao* (a Chinese bun) cradles sliced roast pork tenderloin with smoky miso spread; a main-course lobster is served cold in bite-sized slices with shavings of black truffle. Desserts are sinfully rich.

Kouun—good fortune: there's a valet parking lot next door!

Il Buco

015

Italian ✗✗

107 N. Robertson Blvd. (at Wilshire Blvd.)

Phone: 310-657-1345
Web: www.giacominodrago.com
Prices: $$

Mon – Sat lunch & dinner
Sun dinner only

The cuisine is authentically Old Country traditional, prepared with skill and generosity, setting the family-friendly ambience in what looks to be a typical Italian trattoria, complete with racks of wine bottles and jars of homemade preserves on display. On a warm day, looking in past the sidewalk tables and opened doors through the dining rooms, you could be in any of a hundred Italian cities, right down to the white-paper-draped tables, each topped with a bottle of olive oil.

So too with the fare, which is tasty and casual, sticking to the tried and true. Fried calamari, for instance, is accompanied by a fresh, mild tomato sauce, and pappardelle is traditionally rendered with a ragù of minced meat, slices of Italian sausage and mushrooms.

Il Cielo

 016

9018 Burton Way (at Doheny Dr.)

Phone:	310-276-9990
Web:	www.ilcielo.com
Prices:	$$$

Mon – Sat lunch & dinner

The lovely flowered, shrubbery-sheltered, shaded dining patio and rustic dining areas inside "The Sky" impart a secret-garden feel outdoors and a romantic country-cottage ambience indoors, all enhanced by friendly, attentive service.

Lunch and dinner share refined versions of traditional Italian favorites using fresh seasonal ingredients. At lunch, you could make a meal out of the substantial antipasti, and main courses day and night are sumptuously pastoral as well as generous. Their ingredients harmonize in a lovely symphony of flavors—as in ravioli filled with subtly fragrant porcini mushrooms, coated with melted sage butter and topped with roasted butternut squash. For dessert, tiramisú follows a signature recipe from Italy.

Il Pastaio

017

400 N. Cañon Dr. (at Brighton Way)

Phone:	310-205-5444
Web:	www.giacominodrago.com
Prices:	$$

Lunch & dinner daily

A prime corner location at Cañon Drive and Brighton Way, along with local renown for translucent risotto prepared to order, and delicious pasta handmade on-site account for this rustic trattoria's high-fashion star patronage and curbside luxury-car conga lines. Yet prices are modest (aside from a special truffle menu), servings are bounteous, and the service unpretentious despite the Hollywood power dining here.

Risotto *funghi*, cooked al dente with truffle cheese fondue and earthy wild mushrooms, and a choice of carpaccio (beef, bigeye tuna or swordfish) set the house standard for an unstinting devotion to flavor in this member of chef Giacomino Drago's LA restaurant empire. Like everything else here, traditional *dolci* aim to please.

Beverly Hills

Mako

018

A s i a n ✕✕

225 S. Beverly Dr. (at Charleville Blvd.)

Phone:	310-288-8338	Mon – Fri lunch & dinner
Web:	www.makorestaurant.com	Sat dinner only
Prices:	$$	

The humble potsticker rises to another level here, as your taste buds will tell you (think golden-brown roasted duck versions sparked by fresh ginger, garlic and green scallions, and finished with a dollop of smoky plum sauce). Similarly, sweet lobster anointed with a garlic-scented black-bean sauce rests atop fluffy white rice flavored by the drippings.

Locals looking for fine, low-fuss dining account for much of the patronage of this little spot, removed from the tourist crush. They come to share small plates, especially market-fresh sushi and sashimi at small tables or the kitchen bar. Any menu mysteries are quickly solved by attentive servers.

Take a date for dinner; by night, votive candles cast an intimate aura over the dining room.

Massimo

I t a l i a n ✕✕

019

9513 South Santa Monica Blvd. (at Rodeo Dr.)

Phone:	310-273-7588	Lunch & dinner daily
Web:	www.massimobh.com	
Prices:	$$$	

Fashionistas who lunch take time-outs here, careening off Rodeo Drive with shopping bags and plopping onto chairs in the small, inviting, palm-shaded patio. Watching them is part of the fun, along with sampling copious dishes using local ingredients that impart contemporary California traits to Old World recipes.

The grimly svelte might go no further than the antipasti; mini-entrées in spirit, they encompass eggplant baked with mozzarella and tomato sauce, and beef carpaccio with enough arugula and shaved parmesan to qualify. High culinary craft produces gems like zesty pappardelle sautéed with fresh herb-and-garlic-spiced homemade chicken sausage, the pasta coated with basil pesto. Pay particular attention to the expertly prepared desserts.

Mastro's

S t e a k h o u s e ✗✗✗

020

246 N. Cañon Dr. (bet. Clifton & Dayton Ways)

Phone: 310-888-8782
Web: www.mastrosteakhouse.com
Prices: $$$$

Dinner daily

Traditional, with an attentive staff serving large portions of well-prepared classics, this is a favorite among the local chic, who range from neighbors and business people to A-list celebrities and their circles. The small downstairs bar and the formal, dimly lighted dining room's carved paneled ceilings, closely spaced white-linen-covered tables and black leather banquettes evoke Europe. Upstairs, the bar and casual dining area are more lively.

The bill of fare honors the steakhouse canon. Crab cakes? Of course, atop greens with a creamy lemon sauce. A Porterhouse? Natch, a big one served solo on the plate. Generous sides, cherished Yankee fare, include cheesy potatoes au gratin and sautéed sliced mushrooms and bell peppers. Hail, meat!

Mirü8691

A s i a n ✗✗

022

9162 W. Olympic Blvd. (at S. Palm Dr.)

Phone: 310-777-8378
Web: www.miru8691.com
Prices: $$

Mon – Fri lunch & dinner
Sat – Sun dinner only

Serving Japanese cuisine fused with other Asian styles, this newcomer in a strip mall storefront strives for a funky eclecticism in details like mismatched colored chopsticks, bright neon lights and high-volume techno-club music.

Hip and casual does not define the food, however, which is carefully prepared and elegantly presented. Deft, light touches respect tradition, as in a cube of tofu in flaky tempura batter, dashed with sweet soy sauce; or a nutty miso-flavored broth poured tableside into a bowl of fresh enoki mushrooms, seaweed julienne and sliced chives.

After your meal, the server might ask to snap your picture to add to the sizeable collection of diners already posted on the walls. Of course, you can politely decline.

Matsuhisa ✿

129 N. La Cienega Blvd. (bet. Clifton Way & Wilshire Blvd.)

Phone: 310-659-9639
Web: www.nobumatsuhisa.com
Prices: $$$$

Mon – Fri lunch & dinner
Sat – Sun dinner only

Matsuhisa

Beverly Hills

Tables and sushi-bar seats at Nobu Matsuhisa's first U.S. venture are booked well in advance, making reservations imperative. No wonder. The skill of this chef (who is often in the kitchen here) is legendary, and sushi selections define the cuisine.

À la carte options and tasting menus change nightly. What doesn't change is the expert preparation using the freshest possible ingredients, masterful combinations of flavors and textures, and presentations delightful to the eye. Thus a round disk of finely minced raw salmon is topped with black caviar and chives, served with spicy wasabi-soy sauce. Halibut sashimi lies on grilled scallion and is drizzled with citrus-infused olive oil.

Warm greetings emanate from the staff as you enter the small dining room, where the sushi chefs and black-clad servers create a calming atmosphere despite closely spaced black-lacquered tables.

Appetizers
- Tiradito Nobu Style
- White Fish Sashimi with Dried Miso
- Yellowtail Sashimi with Jalapeño

Entrées
- Black Cod in Miso
- Japanese Kobe Beef Toban-Yaki
- Santa Barbara Filo with Spicy Garlic Sauce

Desserts
- Bento Box
- Trio of Crèmes Brûlées
- Banana Spring Roll

Mr Chow

023

344 N. Camden Dr. (bet. Brighton Way & Wilshire Blvd.)

Phone:	310-278-9911
Web:	www.mrchow.com
Prices:	$$$$

Mon – Fri lunch & dinner
Sat – Sun dinner only

Epitome of a hip-for-the-moment LA dining hotspot, Mr Chow caters to an A-list of celebrities. Expect the entrance to be lined with paparazzi on a perpetual star search. So, if you're dining late and you have The Look, prepare to be blinded by a hail of camera flashes by a fleet-fingered cadre of photographers who shoot first and ask questions later.

Expensive Chinese cuisine rambles from lettuce wraps filled with chicken and veggies to spicy-sweet chile prawns. To accommodate the fickle tastes of the glitterati, Mr Chow's tasting menu differs per table. And while you may not find stars on your plate, you'll find plenty in the chic black and white dining room.

If you've been waiting for a place to wear those designer duds, this is it.

Nic's

024

453 N. Cañon Dr. (at South Santa Monica Blvd.)

Phone:	310-550-5707
Web:	www.nicsbeverlyhills.com
Prices:	$$$

Mon – Sat dinner only

A self-proclaimed shrine to vodka and the martini, Nic's splashy Fifties décor evokes notions of Rat Pack coolness. That can lead to occasional displays of self reverential behavior by the terminally trendy in the white faux-leather banquettes, but the overall friendliness of the place compensates for any posturing engendered in wannabes by all those Silver Bullets.

The kitchen, however, is earnest and eclectic, with a Mediterranean bent. Nic's knack with modern cuisine comes to the fore in steamed Parisian gnocchi in a tasty creamy wine sauce with earthy morels, followed by seared pommery-crusted free-range chicken over a flavorful ratatouille-style bed of multicolored Asian slaw. Wines by the glass keep pace with the well-prepared dishes.

Piccolo Paradiso

025

Italian

150 S. Beverly Dr. (at Wilshire Blvd.)

Phone:	310-271-0030	Mon – Fri lunch & dinner
Web:	www.giacominodrago.com	Sat – Sun dinner only
Prices:	**$$$**	

Part of chef/owner Giacomino Drago's LA empire, which currently encompasses five other area restaurants (including Il Pastaio and Il Buco, also in Beverly Hills), Piccolo Paradiso is indeed a "little paradise." A sleek, modern décor highlighted by polished woods, mirrors and jewel tones befits the chic Beverly Hills crowd that comes here for perfectly prepared and presented Italian fare.

The kitchen strives to find the best produce, meats and other ingredients, and their diligence pays off in savory pastas and wonderfully balanced dishes such as halibut with mango salsa, veal marsala, and the signature risotto with porcini mushrooms and mascarpone cheese. An appealing selection of Italian varietals rounds out the offerings.

Polo Lounge

026

Californian

9641 Sunset Blvd. (bet. Beverly & Cresent Drs.)

Phone:	310-887-2777	Lunch & dinner daily
Web:	www.thebeverlyhillshotel.com	
Prices:	**$$$$**	

In 1941 this restaurant was renamed to honor polo players such as Will Rogers, Darryl Zanuck and Spencer Tracy, who often came here after matches. The Polo Lounge, a metaphor for the food-fueled deal-making at the core of the entertainment trade, shares the Beverly Hills Hotel's *(see hotel listing)* trademark pink and green motif and retro California style, right down to the white wrought-iron tables and chairs on the tree-shaded brick patio.

The menu reflects California's embrace of many cuisines: an Ahi tuna tartare topped with mango and firm *tobiko* caviar, and dripped with citrus-infused chile oil; grilled swordfish topped with a creamy garlic aïoli and a slice of smoky Italian bacon. Desserts are deliciously fancy, like most everything here.

Porta Via

Californian

027

424 N. Cañon Dr. (at South Santa Monica Blvd.)

Phone:	310-274-6534
Web:	N/A
Prices:	$$

Tue – Fri lunch & dinner
Sat – Mon lunch only

Despite its location at a restaurant-rich Beverly Hills crossroad, Porta Via succeeds in being a convivial neighborhood bistro. Here, the percentage of patrons sporting Dolce & Gabbana sunglasses seems a bit lower than in other eateries in the Golden Triangle bounded by Wilshire and Santa Monica boulevards and Cañon Drive.

Locals come here for breakfast, lunch and dinner. In the morning, scones and pastries go down well with a cup of espresso—as heady and strong as any you'd find in Milan. At dinnertime, the cornucopia of lunch salads and sandwiches gives way to simply prepared entrées.

Seating is limited to about a dozen tables inside and a few more out on the sidewalk terrace, where you can take in the tony street scene.

The Prime Grill

Steakhouse

028

421 N. Rodeo Dr. (at Brighton Way)

Phone:	310-860-1233
Web:	www.theprimegrill.com
Prices:	$$$

Mon – Thu lunch & dinner
Fri lunch only
Sun dinner only

A steakhouse keeping Kosher is nothing new in thriving Jewish communities, but this one, which has a sibling in Manhattan, is unusual in featuring both steakhouse fare and sushi. That Kosher is compatible with culinary traditions having no original link to Kosher offerings is appetizingly demonstrated by a Fire Dragon roll of spicy minced tuna wrapped with sushi rice and avocado slices sprinkled with lemon juice. The Grill's wines are *mevushal*, retaining their religious purity no matter who opens, pours or drinks them, a welcoming gesture to all.

On the below-street Garden Level of the Rodeo Collection complex, the Grill's contemporary dining room and cabana-covered outdoor patio offer a respite from Rodeo Drive's high-end mercantile buzz.

The Restaurant at Hotel Bel-Air

 029

French

701 Stone Canyon Rd. (off Sunset Blvd.)

Phone:	310-472-5234
Web:	www.hotelbelair.com
Prices:	**$$$$**

Lunch & dinner daily

The curving lane from Sunset Boulevard through the imposing gates of the Hotel Bel-Air *(see hotel listing)* into Stone Canyon delivers you to a bucolic arboretum where the hotel hides. French doors in the elegantly old-fashioned dining room open onto a terrace whose banquettes are the turf of Hollywood deal-makers, where players huddle in the heady thrall of possibility. A pianist tickles the ivories in the clubby lounge, and a fireplace often crackles.

All this would be window-dressing if it were not for the kitchen's California-flavored French classicism. Dishes like a sautéed fillet of flaky Mediterranean snapper lying on a bed of diced braised leek demonstrate skill. International in scope, the sommelier's selection spotlights rare vintages.

The Stinking Rose

 031

Italian

55 N. La Cienega Blvd. (at Wilshire Blvd.)

Phone:	310-652-7673
Web:	www.thestinkingrose.com
Prices:	**$$**

Lunch & dinner daily

"A Garlic Restaurant," proclaims—and warns—the sign outside. But the well-finished cuisine in this sometimes kitschy shrine to *allium sativum* is not as aggressively devotional as you might expect—although one might question a martini served with two toothpick-skewered cloves

That said, garlic is everywhere, though not in excess. Every celebration of it is generously presented in a hearty rustic recipe. *Bagna calda* is defined as "garlic soaking in a hot tub," and three large pieces of rabbit (leg, rack and breast) come well roasted, crisp on top and tender inside, on a pungent sauce made of olive oil, olives, and of course the stinking rose, with a side of herb and garlic purée. Sheer curiosity makes a scoop of garlic ice cream a popular coda.

Spago ❀❀

030

Californian 🍴🍴🍴

176 N. Cañon Dr. (at Wilshire Blvd.)

Phone: 310-385-0880
Web: www.wolfgangpuck.com
Prices: $$$$

Mon – Sat lunch & dinner
Sun dinner only

Spago Beverly Hills

Located near some of the world's most luxurious shopping, Wolfgang Puck's flagship deserves its storied reputation. Although this celebrity chef runs in many directions, he still finds time to supervise Spago's kitchen. Look for him making rounds in the dining room, which rises to a striking pyramidal skylight.

Epitomizing Californian cuisine in terms of their perfect products, Puck's terrific dishes hit global high notes in silky steamed black bass Hong Kong style (served over a sauté of *choi sum*, snap peas and water chestnuts), or Wiener Schnitzel—Puck's specialty and one of the Austrian chef's childhood favorites—its veal scallop smooth and tender under a golden, crispy crust. Pulling it all together is an outstanding list of reasonably priced domestic and international wines.

The Hollywood A-List likes to dine on the lovely outdoor courtyard, amid trees wrapped with twinkling lights.

Appetizers

- Chino Farms Beet Salad with Goat Cheese, Hazelnuts and Shallot-Citrus Vinaigrette

- Austrian White Asparagus with Yuzu-Miso Vinaigrette, Upland Cress, Favas and Baby Beets

Entrées

- Steamed Black Bass "Hong Kong" Style with Ginger, Garlic, Chili and Bok Choy

- Pan-roasted Liberty Farms Duck Breast with Morels, Ramps and Sweet Pea Flan

Desserts

- "*Kaiserschmarren*" Crème Fraîche Soufflée Pancake with Sautéed Chino Ranch Strawberries

- 12 Layers of Flourless Chocolate Cake with Mocha Praline Cream and Chocolate Sorbet

Sushi & Kushi Imai

J a p a n e s e

8300 Wilshire Blvd. (at San Vicente Blvd.)

Phone: 323-655-2253
Web: www.sushiandkushiimai.com
Prices:

Mon – Fri lunch & dinner
Sat – Sun dinner only

Kushi are skewers for holding food for grilling. Here, they pierce barbecued delicacies like whitefish dripped with lemon, teriyaki marinated chicken, or green Japanese peppers. The restaurant's name honors Takeo Imai, who helped introduce Los Angeles to Tokyo-style nigiri sushi—the kind most familiar to Americans—featuring small amounts of seafood on seasoned rice, originally made and served on the spot by pushcart vendors.

Not bound by tradition, however, the house offers its own recipes, including a California roll packed with fresh shredded crab, cubes of ripe avocado, cucumber sticks and toasted *nori* (tissue-thin marine algae) wrapped in sticky white rice flavored with rice-wine vinegar and toasted sesame seeds. *Imai-sensei* would approve.

Sushi Dokoro Ki Ra La

J a p a n e s e

9777 South Santa Monica Blvd. (at Wilshire Blvd.)

Phone: 310-275-9003
Web: www.sushikirala.com
Prices: **$$**

Mon – Fri lunch & dinner
Sat – Sun dinner only

Light floods through the front glass wall, yet the small interior, with spare walls and simple tables and chairs, sustains an air of calm in this fashionable fishbowl of a sushi house.

Omakase (chef's choice) options at lunch and dinner offer diners the full flower of his skill using the best ingredients of the day. Anything leafy is crisp from the garden and artfully seasoned with touches like a miso-based vinaigrette. Fresh fluke and whitefish are garnished with sliced scallions and grated ginger. Yellowtail might be punched up with a daub of fresh, horseradish-like wasabi. The maestro here is not afraid to seriously spice a tuna roll, in this case with chile, scallion and a side of pickled ginger. The quality belies his modest prices.

Beverly Hills

Sushi House Unico

Japanese

034

2932 1/2 Beverly Glen Circle (at Beverly Glen Blvd.)

Phone:	310-474-2740	Mon – Fri lunch & dinner
Web:	www.shusushi.com	Sat – Sun dinner only
Prices:		

Another bold venture by chef Giacomino Drago (of Il Pastaio), Shu (as it's known) fuses Japanese and Latin flavors in a brown-hued modern space in the Beverly Glen shopping center. A haven for well-heeled Bel-Air ladies who lunch, the dining space incorporates a contemporary Japanese sensibility with lots of natural elements (stone, wood, bamboo) and bright red accents. There is fusion here. Ahi tuna in jalapeño and ginger sauce with Japanese risotto certainly qualifies, as do the signature Shu tacos—creamy ripe avocado, ground raw tuna, shredded crab meat and a fresh prawn tucked inside crispy fried wonton-like wrappers. Most dishes, including first-quality sushi, hover closer to Japanese technique and taste.
Both valet and self-parking apply.

Sushi Sushi

Japanese

035

326 1/2 S. Beverly Dr. (bet. Gregory Way & Olympic Blvd.)

Phone:	310-277-1165	Mon – Fri lunch & dinner
Web:	N/A	Sat dinner only
Prices:		

"Serious about Sushi" might be the online moniker of fans of this out-of-the-way hole-in-the-wall where traditional sushi rules. Dimly lit behind wooden slat blinds, the narrow dining room has scant decoration save reed mats covering the ceiling. There is no scene here, no tinkering with time-tested methods for preparing sushi and sashimi.
The chefs prefer to call the shots, *omakase*-style, at lunch—offering a sushi combination (soup, salad and dessert) that changes daily based on what's available and fresh from the catches of tuna, mackerel, yellowtail, salmon, prawns and more. Add wines by the glass and modest prices, and dinner reservations are a must.
Arrive ahead of time, for parking spaces are usually scarce.

208 Rodeo

Californian

036

208 Via Rodeo (at Wilshire Blvd.)

Phone:	310-275-2428	Lunch & dinner daily
Web:	www.208rodeo.com	
Prices:	$$$	

When you want lunch on the terrace, make a beeline for Via Rodeo. Boasting one of the best dining terraces around, 208 Rodeo offers prime people-watching from its always-packed patio that peers out on a charming lane of chic shops off Rodeo Drive.

A bowl of chilled gazpacho makes a refreshing start to a summer lunch, while California accents flavor light entrées such as grilled mahi mahi served with Israeli couscous and a sweet salsa made from mango and papaya. Even mac 'n cheese goes upscale here, with the addition of Shelton Farms free-range chicken, conchiglie pasta, prosciutto and black truffles; for foodies-in-training, the kids menu includes a mini Kobe burger.

A short list of breakfast fare accommodates shoppers as well as shopkeepers.

Vibrato

American

038

2930 Beverly Glen Circle (at Beverly Glen Blvd.)

Phone:	310-474-9400	Tue – Sun dinner only
Web:	www.vibratogrilljazz.com	
Prices:	$$$$	

With its tables and banquettes arranged to afford clear views of a stage where first-rate jazz musicians perform nightly, some might ask if as much attention is paid to the food. The answer is yes. Up in the Bel-Air hills, Vibrato's swanky interior mixes elements of a posh recording studio and an eclectic art gallery.

Part supper club, part steakhouse, it ventures skillfully into seafood, chicken, and even lamb dishes. A filet mignon is grilled to order and paired with a creamy sauce and some onion here, some blue cheese there. You see the balance in the sides: herbed shoestring French fries versus grilled buttery broccolini topped with toasted almonds and grated Parmigiano Reggiano. The wine list includes some unsung yet exceptional labels.

Urasawa ✿✿

037

218 N. Rodeo Dr. (at Wilshire Blvd.)

Phone:	310-247-8939	Mon – Sat dinner only
Web:	N/A	
Prices:	**$$$$**	

Beverly Hills

Urasawa

There's no sign outside, and inside only ten stools face a sushi bar for which there is no menu. An elevator lifts guests from the garage valet parking to the Rodeo Collection's second floor and a discreet curtained entrance.

Inside, chef Hiroyuki "Hiro" Urasawa chats with guests at the L-shaped sushi bar. Traditionally dressed servers never leave your side, taking instruction from the master in Japanese.

The point is to celebrate this singular cuisine. A carved turnip mimics a chrysanthemum bud, its hollowed center filled with a fragrant garlic and ginger shrimp paste. Cubes of Wagyu beef cooked in smoky-sweet ponzu sauce fall apart on the tongue. Sushi placed atop warm rice mixed with grated wasabi must be eaten within ten seconds, instructs the chef, lest the rice heat the raw fish. And so on, for three unforgettable hours at the summit of the sushi arts in Los Angeles.

Appetizers

- Uni Nikogori: Terrine of Sea Urchin, White Shrimp, Shiso, Mountain Potato and Gelatin from Fish.
- Junsai "Shot" with Myoga, Shiso, Negi and Yuzu Zest

Entrées

- Chef's Sashimi Selection on Carved Ice with Pickles and Edible Garnishes
- Kinuta Maki of Snapper, Shrimp, Shiso, Takuan and Myoga with Pickled Daikon, Nori and Ponzu

Desserts

- Sesame Seed Ice Cream
- Grapefruit "Jello" with Goji Berries

Domaines
Ott ★

Sharing the nature of infinity

Route du Fort-de-Brégançon - 83250 La Londe-les-Maures - Tél. 33 (0)4 94 01 53 53
Fax 33 (0)4 94 01 53 54 - domaines-ott.com - ott.particuliers@domaines-ott.com

Greater Downtown

Chinatown, Koreatown

Within the eight square miles bounded by Chinatown, the Los Angeles River, the University of Southern California (USC) and Western Avenue, Downtown LA is a reviving inner city enjoying the return of nightlife. Until the 1980s, Downtown dining meant a vintage steakhouse or a cafeteria. (The nation's first cafeteria opened here in the late 1800s, adopting the Spanish term for coffeehouse.) Today LA's Downtown claims some of the city's finest restaurants and cultural venues, including the Music Center, the Walt Disney Concert Hall, and the Museum of Contemporary Art. A 1981 ordinance legalizing artists/ squatters in vacant warehouse space on the east side created the **Arts District**, a community of studio lofts and galleries.

An Urban Renaissance

Where settlers staked out the farming village that became Los Angeles in 1781, the 44-acre **El Pueblo** Historical Monument now preserves its oldest building, Avila Adobe, in the Olvera Street marketplace. Nearby Chinatown, founded in the 1930s by those displaced when Union Station was built, holds family-run shops, dim sum parlors, jewelers and galleries. **Little Tokyo**, center of LA's Japanese community, retains many original 19th-century buildings—not to mention some good sushi.

Southern California's first oil well was drilled northeast of Downtown in 1892. By 1897 there were 500 wells in the area, overseen by a mercantile elite who rode the Angels

Flight funicular railway to Victorian manses crowning Bunker Hill. Spring Street, the self-proclaimed Wall Street of the West in the 20th century, boasts a rare unbroken string of pre-1931 buildings. The **Broadway Theater District** holds a dozen pre-World War II movie houses; the refurbished Orpheum is still active.

Grand Central Market at 317 Broadway has sold fresh fruits, vegetables, meats, poultry and fish since 1917. Hub of the West's apparel trade, the **Fashion District** (bounded by I-10 and Main, 7th and San Pedro streets) caters to bargain hunters and wholesale buyers. The vast Flower Mart centers around 8th Street, while 3,000 dealers in the **Jewelry District** (most along

Olive and Broadway between 5th and 8th streets) offer competitive prices.

ASIAN INFLUENCE

A fixture in LA since the mid-1800's, LA's Chinese population today is concentrated in **Chinatown,** a Downtown district marked by dim sum parlors, food markets, Taoist temples and curio shops. An influx of South Koreans in the 1960s transformed the languishing Wilshire Center district, though Latinos and African Americans still outnumber Asians here. Restaurants in **Koreatown** dish up authentic fare, while its bars and attract hipsters.

Blue Velvet

Contemporary

001

750 S. Garland Ave. (at 7th St.)

Phone:	213-239-0061	Mon – Fri lunch & dinner
Web:	www.bluevelvetrestaurant.com	Sat – Sun dinner only
Prices:	$$	

Take the name of a retro pop-song hit and a cult film; find a former Holiday Inn with skyline views through floor-to-ceiling windows; design it to the max of Minimalism with "eco-friendly" wood, stone and iron; make restrooms unisex; serve late; and you have arguably achieved critical mass in LA-style hipness.

Offer a refined, seasonal menu featuring some American classics and smartly updated French and Asian dishes, and you have a standout in this western fringe of Downtown that's still in the early stage of gentrification.

Asian influences appear, as in a crispy, tender Kurobuta pork-cube appetizer in a sweet-and-sour sauce; chicken confit with a romaine, avocado, tomato and blue-cheese salad is a French affair. All this, and a parking lot in front.

Cafe Pinot

Contemporary

002

700 W. 5th St. (at Flower St.)

Phone:	213-239-6500	Mon – Fri lunch & dinner
Web:	www.patinagroup.com	Sat – Sun dinner only
Prices:	$$$	

You couldn't ask for a more ideal location Downtown, overlooking Maguire Gardens' terraces and fountains, unveiled in the 1920s as the grand entrance to the Los Angeles Central Library. The twin dining rooms' ceiling-high windows frame skyscrapers, but the best seats are on the outdoor patio—a rose-edged oasis by day, a romantic lair by night.

Fish-market specials may feature sashimi, and pan-seared or grilled bass, cod or salmon, while filet mignon, rotisserie chicken and Colorado lamb are regular entrées. The wine list is well chosen, as are the cheeses (Petit Basque, anyone?), an alternative to tantalizing desserts.

If you don't take advantage of the cafe's valet parking, there's two-hour validated parking in the library, off Flower Street.

Checkers Downtown

 C a l i f o r n i a n

535 S. Grand Ave. (bet. 5th & 6th Sts.)

Phone: 213-624-0000
Web: www.checkershotel.com
Prices: $$$

Lunch & dinner daily

Tucked inside the boutique Hilton Checkers Hotel, this Financial District hideaway sports a clubby ambience equally suited to serious business or earnest romancing. Credit the interior's warm colors, fine fabrics, comfy seating, English china and soft jazz. A heated patio offers sheltered open-air dining.

One of the best options Downtown for lunch, dinner or Sunday brunch, Checkers serves refined Californian cuisine with Asian, Italian and French accents. Dessert brings perennial favorites like crème brûlée and bread pudding. And at lunchtime the friendly waitstaff respects diners' time limits with snap-to-it efficiency.

A pre-theater dinner package includes complimentary town-car service to nearby venues, including Disney Hall.

Cicada

 C o n t e m p o r a r y

617 S. Olive St. (bet. 6th & 7th Sts.)

Phone: 213-488-9488
Web: www.cicadarestaurant.com
Prices: $$$$

Mon – Sat dinner only

Back when hats were de rigueur in America, a year before the Crash of 1929, a high-fashion haberdashery opened in this Art Deco space. And space this haberdashery-turned-restaurant has: 15,000 square feet on two levels, permitting widely spaced tables that—especially on the mezzanine—manage to seem private under 30-foot-high ceilings.

Italian-Asian fusion (the chef is Korean) defines dishes like Pacific tuna tartare with soba noodles and salmon roe, while Mediterranean-style pastas assert Roman influences. French sensibilities, particularly in sauces, add sophistication to meat and fish entrées, and a market-priced grilled fish special is offered daily. Refined service makes Cicada popular for romantic tête-à-têtes and private events.

Greater Downtown

Empress Pavilion

005

Chinese

988 N. Hill St. (at Bernard St.)

Phone:	213-617-9898	Lunch & dinner daily
Web:	www.empresspavilion.com	
Prices:		

An encyclopedic choice of dim sum and Mandarin Szechwan specialties draws a largely Asian crowd to this Chinatown emporium whose popularity with locals can mean a long wait for a table. Adjoining the picturesque Bamboo Plaza, the big banquet-style dining room is noisy but table service is quick, with cart-pushing waitresses offering an endless stream of courses such as pork buns, beef meatballs, dried-shrimp rice noodles, and sticky rice wrapped in a lotus leaf.

The regular menu lists dozens of traditional favorites like fried noodle and rice dishes, and stir-fried beef with ginger and onion, along with shark-fin soup and Peking duck. Sharing courses, family style, is the best way to sample the enticing variety of dishes.

Izayoi

006

Japanese

132 S. Central Ave. (bet. 1st & 2nd Sts.)

Phone:	213-613-9554	Mon – Fri lunch & dinner
Web:	N/A	Sat dinner only
Prices:	$$	

Authentic Japanese cuisine beautifully presented and modestly priced makes this Little Tokyo strip-mall place stand out. The changing menu reflects the abundance of a nearby wholesale fish market and lists traditional grilled, simmered, fried or steamed fish and meat dishes; more exotic fare includes spicy yam cake, monkfish liver, and grilled dried stingray fin. Sushi flown in direct from Japan is slightly more expensive, but worth the price.

At lunch, the first 20 diners may order a low-priced house "box" lunch (not to go). In the evening, sushi combinations, tuna sashimi and grilled entrées highlight the dinner menu. Serving sizes are modest, so order a variety and share.

To ensure a seat at the small sushi bar, reserve well ahead.

J Lounge

007

C a l i f o r n i a n

1119 S. Olive St. (bet. 11th & 12th Sts.)

Phone:	213-746-7746	Mon – Fri lunch & dinner
Web:	www.jloungela.com	Sat dinner only
Prices:	$$	

The frisson of big ideas is palpable in many LA debuts, from films to restaurants like this 25,000-square-foot newcomer. Boasting California cuisine, live entertainment, a humidor, and a patio with private VIP cabanas, J-Lounge attracts young film and media types who fancy that whatever they wear is fashionable and wherever they land is hip. But this place delivers more than attitude. Its post-Modern décor, dramatic lighting and exposed brick walls suit the wide-ranging menu, which melds American favorites with Californian flair. Soups, risotto and fish entrées change daily.

With its signature cocktails and menu of pizzas, charcuterie and tuna tartare, the sexy lounge is the place to schmooze, smooch or party until the wee hours of the night.

Nick & Stef's Steakhouse

008

S t e a k h o u s e

330 S. Hope St. (bet. 3rd & 4th Sts.)

Phone:	213-680-0330	Mon – Fri lunch & dinner
Web:	www.patinagroup.com	Sat – Sun dinner only
Prices:	$$$	

A classic steakhouse, Nick & Stef's dishes up unabashedly hearty food in a pair of modern woodsy-warm rooms and on an open-air terrace. From ribeyes to veal cheeks, this place worships prime dry-aged beef, but organic chicken, wild salmon, lamb chops and even free-range buffalo co-star. Daily specials tout seafood and pasta.

A classic Caesar prepared tableside tops the salad list, which includes salt-roasted baby beets tossed with walnuts and goat cheese, as well as a seared-tuna Niçoise. Pumpkin and butternut-squash hash, broccoli rabe, and braised beans with prosciutto raise the bar on steakhouse sides.

The restaurant offers two-hour validated parking in the building and a complimentary shuttle to the Music Center and the Staples Center.

Greater Downtown

Noé

009

Contemporary

251 S. Olive St. (at 2nd St.)

Phone: 213-356-4100

Dinner daily

Web: www.noerestaurant.com

Prices: $$$

Noé heralds its food as "progressive American cuisine," melding a strong Japanese influence with a French sensibility. "Progressive" implies change, and the menu does, constantly, along ingenious but disciplined lines. Yuzu Kosho chicken with Sansai rice, risotto-stuffed quail cooked *sous vide*, and roasted Scottish salmon with citrus fava-bean purée will give you the picture.

Its location, in the Omni Hotel *(see hotel listing)* next to the Walt Disney Concert Hall and the Museum of Contemporary Art, makes Noé a natural for a pre-theater nosh. But with stylish service, more than 100 foreign wines, a well-stocked humidor and a "cigar-friendly" outdoor patio, this is a place to linger, rathen than rush through en route to a performance.

Park's Barbeque

010

Korean

955 S. Vermont Ave. (at San Marino St.)

Phone: 213-380-1717

Lunch & dinner daily

Web: N/A

Prices: 🍴

Park's location in an undistinguished Koreatown mall makes it easy to overlook this authentic restaurant. Inside, however, is a large, clean, well-ventilated space of black-granite tables equipped with charcoal grills. Young servers are knowledgeable and friendly.

Start with the *pan chan* appetizers, a variety of little dishes such as tofu and vegetables seasoned with cabbage condiment and garlic. You can grill Kobe beef, marinated pork belly and other meats to your taste. A spicy beef stew with seasonal vegetables comes with sticky rice. Chef's specials may offer hearty portions of items like a seafood pancake, beef leg tendons, and pickled raw Dungeness crab in soy sauce.

There's a very small fee for valet parking at lunch and dinner.

Patina ✿

141 S. Grand Ave. (at 2nd St.)

Phone:	213-972-3331	Tue – Fri lunch & dinner
Web:	www.patinagroup.com	Sat – Sun dinner only
Prices:	$$$$	

Patina Restaurant Group

To open a restaurant in the Walt Disney Concert Hall is akin to stepping onto the stage at the Los Angeles Philharmonic, also resident in this Frank Gehry landmark: you're assumed to be the best and expected to please a sophisticated audience. Like the hall's maestro and musicians, Joachim Splichal and his professional staff stay on key, raising Patina into the City of Angels' highest registers.

A seasonally sensitive menu presents the familiar in unusual ways—a lobster sausage; a wild buffalo tenderloin; a baba au rhum with grapefruit sorbet and a mascarpone emulsion. Like the concerts next door, everything, from caviar starters to bottles on the outstanding wine list, is elegantly presented and reinterpreted.

At lunch, Patina features several prix-fixe menus as well as an à la carte selection. The same is true at dinner, when reservations are imperative—especially for concert nights.

Appetizers	*Entrées*	*Desserts*
● Caviar Guéridon with Traditional Accompaniments	● Côte de Boeuf, Mushroom Ragoût	● Classic French Toast and Poached Apricot Cardamom Crumble
● Maine Lobster Tail with Vanilla-Marinated Pineapple, Mango in Ginger Oil and Toasted Coconut	● Scottish Salmon, Spring Pea Emulsion, Bacon and Corn Ragoût	● Chocolate Tuile and Macadamia Nut Decadence
	● Roasted Loin and Crispy Belly of Berkshire Pork	● Vanilla Panna Cotta and Citrus Salad with a Petite Madeleine

Greater Downtown

Greater Downtown

Royale

012

Contemporary ✗✗

2619 Wilshire Blvd. (at S. Rampart Ave.)

Phone:	213-388-8488	Mon – Fri lunch & dinner
Web:	N/A	Sat – Sun dinner only
Prices:	$$	

This fancy setting raises expectations that are not disappointed. Inside the refurbished Jazz Age Wilshire Royal Hotel (now condos), you'll find a swanky lounge, then two dining areas—a leafy intimate patio and a columned, high-ceilinged, 1920s-era ballroom with its original marble-topped, carved French oak bar, and floorboards on which Fred Astaire reputedly danced.

Californian dishes embellished by international influences and French technique highlight the seasonal menu. Start with the likes of salmon with Kaffir lime, cucumber-onion relish and pink peppercorn, and sea bass carpaccio. Then move on to entrées such as scallops with potato fondue, or Mediterranean-spiced lamb roast with sweet peppers. For dessert, dive into a large bowl of cotton candy.

R 23

013

Japanese ✗✗

923 E. 2nd St. (bet. Alameda St. & Santa Fe Ave.)

Phone:	213-687-7178	Mon – Fri lunch & dinner
Web:	www.r23.com	Sat dinner only
Prices:	$$$	

This "Japanese restaurant+gallery" has won a decade of praise for artfully presenting a broad array of sushi and sashimi on lovely ceramic platters. Honoring tradition, daily chef's specials encompass pine-tree mushroom soup, monkfish liver with ponzu sauce, grilled freshwater eel, and lightly sautéed shimeji mushrooms with chile peppers and *mozuku* (seasoned seaweed). Desserts like tiramisú and green-tea cheesecake exhibit more Western influence.

Inside, the industrial-style décor is chic, the sushi bar convivial, the art fine, and Frank Gehry's cardboard chairs comfy. The exterior is gritty urban: a narrow alley in an erstwhile warehouse district now filled with artists' studios. Valet parking or taxi service is the way to go here.

66

Thousand Cranes

Japanese ✗✗

014

120 S. Los Angeles St. (bet. 1st & 2nd Sts.)

Phone: 213-253-9255
Web: www.newotani.com
Prices: $$

Sun – Fri lunch & dinner
Sat dinner only

Asymmetry, simplicity, austerity, naturalness, calmness, spirituality, subtlety: the seven principles of Zen define this serene restaurant. Located on the garden level (third floor) of the New Otani Hotel in Little Tokyo, Thousand Cranes peers out on a manicured Japanese garden. The garden's waterfall burbles soothingly in the background as you mindfully savor each bite.

Intriguing combinations of sushi, sashimi, soba and tempura are offered at lunch, while evening rolls out a more expansive and pricey menu including chef's special sushi assortments as well as a nine-course *kaiseki* dinner based on the freshest seasonal products.

A favorite haunt of local Japanese business people, the sushi and tempura bars are open at dinnertime only.

Yang Chow

Chinese ✗

016

819 N. Broadway (bet. Alpine & College Sts.)

Phone: 213-625-0811
Web: www.yangchow.com
Prices:

Lunch & dinner daily

Look at Yang Chow's pink façade and its basic décor, and you might conclude that this is a run-of-the-mill Chinatown restaurant. But look again: the line of regulars waiting to order savory Mandarin and Szechwan dishes at this family-run restaurant will tell you a different story.

Traditional fare—wonton soup, noodles and made-to-order spring rolls, as well as seafood, beef, pork and poultry in all their Asian incarnations—fills the menu, and specialties encompass spicy dishes such as Szechwan chicken, slippery shrimp, and Kung Pao fresh conch. Lunch combos and family dinners provide the most bang for the buck.

Visit Yang Chow's two other locations: in Canoga Park *(6443 Topanga Canyon Blvd.)*, and the newest in Pasadena *(3777 E. Colorado Blvd.)*.

Water Grill

Seafood XX X

544 S. Grand Ave. (bet. 5th & 6th Sts.)

Phone:	213-891-0900	Mon – Fri lunch & dinner
Web:	www.watergrill.com	Sat – Sun dinner only
Prices:	$$$$	

Water Grill

A block from Pershing Square and convenient to Downtown theaters, Water Grill nets some of the city's best seafood. An elegant raw bar in the front room makes waves with a wide range of regional oysters and other chilled shellfish. Diners farther back in the lively, wood-paneled main space can drop anchor just outside the action in the open kitchen.

Behind the glass wall, the chef's busy brigade creates swells of satisfaction in the form of creative preparations that play up the clean, bright flavors of the highest-quality fish. Pan-roasted Maryland striped bass, for example, may be laid atop a bed of creamy lemon-scented potato purée to complement the lemon-caper sauce that naps the bass. Alaskan halibut, line-caught wild John Dory, Maine lobster and Pacific bigeye tuna might also appear on the menu, depending on the catch of the day.

Appetizers

- Hamachi, Meyer Lemon, Pea Tendrils, Muscat Grapes
- Dungeness and Blue Crab Cake, Yogurt-Lime-Cucumber
- Soy and Wasabi Marinated Bigeye, Ton Buri, Hijiki

Entrées

- Butter Poached Lobster with Artichoke "Barigoule"
- Sumac-spiced Barramundi with Calamari-Saffron Israeli Couscous

Desserts

- Hazelnut Mousse and Chocolate Dacquoise
- Blood Orange Creamsicle
- Coffee and Lemon Lavender Crèmes Brûlées

Yong Su San

Korean

950 S. Vermont Ave. (at Olympic Blvd.)

Phone:	213-388-3042	Lunch & dinner daily
Web:	N/A	
Prices:	**$$**	

The Korean consular crowd who regularly dines here, quietly fussed over by traditionally costumed hostesses, may prize Yong Su San for its many small private rooms that offer discreet diplomacy. More likely it is the refined and traditional cuisine they favor, especially the set menus for two or more.

What is familiar to Koreans seems exotic to most everyone else, like a clear mungbean-jelly appetizer mixed with mushroom and seaweed, a cold buckwheat-noodle soup, steamed pork with pan-fried green beans, or barbecued sliced short ribs over a bed of onions. You may order à la carte, but know that the chef's tastings are interesting, balanced and abundant. Rolling out up to 20 courses, these set menus dish up a memorable feast fit for an emperor.

Greater Downtown

69

Hollywood
Midtown, West Hollywood

Is any American institution more durable than Hollywood, still a tourist magnet despite the loss of most of its film and TV studios? A 2002 bid failed to incorporate set boundaries claiming about 170,000 residents in a roughly four-mile square between the cities of Beverly Hills, West Hollywood and Burbank, and Melrose Avenue on the south. Since that annexes Los Feliz, Griffith Park and the iconic Hollywood Sign, all claimed by other constituencies, the issue is far from settled.

redevelopment movement began in the 1990s. Proof of its progress is the newly renovated Hollywood Bowl and the return of the **Academy Awards**, first bestowed at the Hollywood Roosevelt Hotel, now permanently ensconced in the new **Kodak Theatre**. Confidence in Hollywood's future has encouraged entrepreneurial chefs and restaurateurs to set up shop in the area's smart new spaces.

THE TOWN THAT MOVIES BUILT

Subdivided in the 1880s by Prohibitionist Horace Wilcox and named by his wife after a friend's country home, Hollywood was an independent city until water shortages compelled its annexation to Los Angeles in 1910. The following year the first movie studio opened on **Sunset Boulevard** at Gower Street, where CBS's former Columbia Square studio now stands. Paramount Pictures began in 1913 in a rented horse barn near Sunset and Vine, moving to its current location a mile south in 1926. Between the world wars the industry boomed, showcasing its product in **Hollywood Boulevard** movie palaces like Grauman's Chinese Theatre *(right)*, El Capitan, and the Egyptian, now home to the American Cinematheque.

By the 1960s, rising land prices were driving production away as urban blight spread. A grassroots

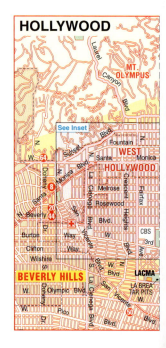

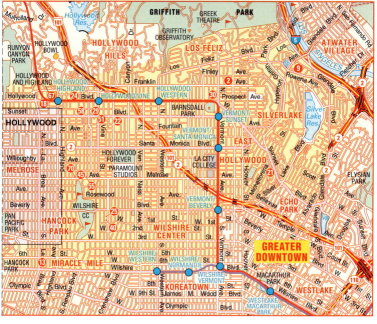

WEST HOLLYWOOD

Beyond the LA city limits and the reach of its vice squads, the neighborhood adjoining Beverly Hills enabled Hollywood's smart set to defy Prohibition and convention in **Sunset Strip** casinos and speakeasies like the Mocambo, the Café Trocadero, and Ciro's (now the Comedy Store), whose Sunday night "tea dances" allowed men to dance together in defiance of city law. Chic residence hotels like the Chateau Marmont attracted an upscale demimonde. Nightlife soared again during the 1960s, when clubs such as Whiskey a Go Go and the Troubadour introduced many music legends. Today the Strip (between Crescent Heights Boulevard and Doheny Drive) boasts rock clubs, restaurants and boutiques with an A-list clientele. Credit the sizeable gay community (about 40 percent of 37,000 residents), which led the 1984 movement to incorporate a city now known for its progressive policies and civic pride.

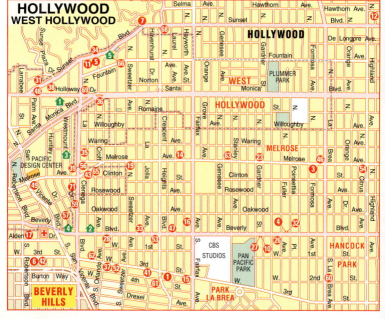

A.O.C.

 001

M e d i t e r r a n e a n

8022 W. 3rd St. (bet. Crescent Heights Blvd. & Edinburgh Ave.)

Phone:	323-653-6359	Dinner daily
Web:	www.aocwinebar.com	
Prices:	$$	

With a name that stands for *Appellation d'Origine Controlée*, the French system for labeling wines, it will come as no surprise that the wine list at A.O.C. is extensive and well selected, available by the bottle or by the glass.

Partners Suzanne Goin and Caroline Styne (of Lucques) designed the list to pair with small plates that run from elegant charcuterie and pork confit to grilled, fried or smoked fish. The bold use of spices, along with bright garnishes like watermelon radish, pomegranate seeds and dandelion greens, enliven the dishes. On average, three plates per person make a meal.

Evenings, you'll find the fashionable noshing in this always-crowded, bi-level haunt that features an outdoor rooftop patio for dining under the stars.

Hollywood

Alcove

 002

A m e r i c a n

1929 Hillhurst Ave. (at Franklin Ave.)

Phone:	323-644-0100	Lunch & dinner daily
Web:	www.alcovecafe.com	
Prices:		

Order at the counter, get a number, and claim a spot in the old bungalow's small room—or even better, sit outside on the redbrick terrace, where you can drink in the aura of Loz Feliz amid greenery and charming steel cafe chairs and tables.

You might have to line up, as Alcove is a hit; locals love the fact that breakfast is served until 2:30pm on weekdays and 4pm on weekends. Soup and salad specials are chalked up daily, and portions are hearty. The house Cobb salad, for instance, is a whopper, accented with Point Reyes blue cheese and applewood-smoked bacon, and served with the bakery's onion bread. The list of gourmet sandwiches runs the gamut of possibilities.

Check out the tempting cakes on display by the counter before you decide on dessert.

All' Angelo

003

7166 Melrose Ave. (bet. Detroit St. & La Brea Ave.)

Phone:	323-933-9540	Mon – Fri lunch & dinner
Web:	www.allangelo.com	Sat dinner only
Prices:	**$$$**	

All' Angelo looks serious, with its creamy yellow walls, hanging blown-glass lamps, impeccable table settings, and soft lighting from wall sconces and candles. And it is, about food and wine at least, attracting a like-minded crowd who come here for the food rather than the scene—a refreshing change on this stretch of Melrose.

Owner Stefano Ongaro (formerly of Valentino and Il Drago) and his Valentino colleague, Mirko Paderno (who starred at Dolce), present an extensive, ambitious menu of antipasti and salad, pasta, fish and meat, carefully selected and well prepared. There are homemade dishes like potatoes Tortelli in a mushroom sauce, and garganelli with braised beef and gaeta olives. The wine list favors Italy over California and France.

Angelini Osteria

004

7313 Beverly Blvd. (at Poinsettia Pl.)

Phone:	323-297-0070	Tue – Fri lunch & dinner
Web:	www.angeliniosteria.com	Sat – Sun dinner only
Prices:	**$$$**	

Good things do come in small packages, like this unpretentious trattoria, one of LA's most popular Italian restaurants. Named after chef/owner Gino Angelini, it serves rustic good food that attracts an A-list clientele who savor signatures like the whole branzino roasted in sea salt and aromatic herbs, and lasagna *verde*, a family recipe made with beef and veal ragù. Specials (roasted leg of pork, veal saltimbocca *alla Romana*) correspond to days of the week.

The warm ambience comes thanks to exposed brick walls, hardwood floors, and welcoming Italian-born waiters. At this osteria, the mood is often boisterous, and the wine list is strong in labels from Piedmont and Tuscany. Seating options include a small sidewalk terrace and a pizza counter.

Asia de Cuba

Fusion

005

8440 Sunset Blvd. (bet. La Cienega Blvd. & Olive Dr.)

Phone:	323-848-6000	Lunch & dinner daily
Web:	www.chinagrillmanagement.com	
Prices:	**$$$**	

Conceived by Jeffrey Chodorow, designed by Philippe Starck, and housed in the chic Mondrian Hotel, Asia de Cuba's sleek white interiors and handsome staff suit its buzz as one of the must-be-seen-there eateries on the Sunset Strip. The swanky outdoor terrace (reserve in advance) offers a sweeping view of the city, amid trellised ficus trees in theatrically oversized pots, an open-sky bar and a pool.

Portions are large and ideal for dining family-style, which is encouraged. The food plays riffs on Thai, Cuban, Chinese and Caribbean cuisine with favorites like tunapica (tuna tartare with Spanish olives, black currants, almonds, coconut and soy-lime vinaigrette) and grilled mojito-glazed strip steak with ginger chickpea fries.

Barefoot

Californian

006

8722 W. 3rd St. (at Robertson Blvd.)

Phone:	310-276-6223	Lunch & dinner daily
Web:	www.barefootrestaurant.com	
Prices:	**$$**	

Though the towers of Cedars-Sinai Hospital loom across the street, an eclectic mix of Asian, Italian and Californian fare and a Mediterranean aura makes Barefoot the neighborhood's top draw for lunch on its outdoor terraces.

Midday diners go for Cobb and Caesar salads, impromptu toss-ups like seared rare Ahi tuna with spicy Asian greens sharpened with soy ginger, and a lunch-only sandwich board offering the likes of portobello mushrooms with roasted peppers and goat cheese. Choices widen at dinner, when a sushi and sashimi bar opens. Otherwise, familiar California fare (wild salmon, rosemary roasted chicken, braised short ribs) balances with surprises like Lake Superior whitefish, and curry jumbo shrimp with coconut sticky rice.

Hollywood

Bar Marmont

007

8221 Sunset Blvd. (bet. Havenhurst Dr. & Marmont Ln.)

Phone:	323-656-0575	Dinner daily
Web:	www.chateaumarmont.com	
Prices:	**$$**	

Long an infamous hideaway for the glitterati, Chateau Marmont looks down on Sunset Strip from its hilltop perch. Bar Marmont's sculpted walls and plush banquettes adjoin a lively lounge area. The vaulted atrium ceiling, dark woods and red-silk lamp shades suit the hotel's castle-like architecture.

Carolynn Spence, from The Spotted Pig in Manhattan, offers a European-influenced menu of comfort food. Here, comfort food means smoked trout topped by crème fraîche atop hollow potatoes filled with capers and onion. Halibut may be kicked up with Romesco sauce and chorizo; gnocchi is made from sheep's-milk ricotta. Lest it all get too haute, there's the "Damn Good Burger" served on a toasted brioche with gruyère and homemade ketchup.

BIN 8945

008

8945 Santa Monica Blvd. (at Robertson Blvd.)

Phone:	310-550-8945	Tue — Sun dinner only
Web:	www.bin8945.com	
Prices:	**$$**	

This intimate bistro specializes in matchmaking wines with food, and the staff will be happy to set you up with a tasting menu, or a five- to seven-course customized feast. The bar stocks 600 wines available by the bottle (with a large choice under $50), plus 70 that are poured by the glass, not to mention sake, beer and port. The menu revolves around the freshest seasonal ingredients, and the chef's spice rack is international in scope. Not sure what wine goes best with porcini-rubbed venison, oysters on the half shell, rabbit lasagna or duck-fat fries? Fear not. You've come to the right place.

Snag a seat on the heated terrace for some prime West Hollywood people-watching day and night; Bin 8945 is open most nights until 2am.

Blair's

009

Californian

2903 Rowena Ave. (bet. Glendale & Hyperion Blvds.)

Phone: 323-660-1882   Lunch & dinner daily
Web: www.blairsrestaurant.com
Prices: $$

Though mostly gentrified by creative sorts, the Silverlake area wasn't known for dining until this convivial neighborhood spot auditioned and won raves. One room stands in as a breakfast, lunch and brunch cafe—mostly salads and burgers, but the former are organic and the latter sirloin—with bare bistro tables and a counter of fresh pastries on display.

The second room plays a more elegant role, serving dinner on white tablecloths amid chocolate-colored walls and soft music. Its more ambitious menu features farm-raised meats such as roasted Calistoga chicken served with red bliss potatoes. Ingredients are fresh, the mood laid-back, and the service efficient.

If you can't find street parking, there's a small lot behind the restaurant.

Hollywood

BLD

010

American

7450 Beverly Blvd. (at N. Vista St.)

Phone: 323-930-9744   Lunch & dinner daily
Web: www.bldrestaurant.com
Prices: $$

Arriving late in a neighborhood with a plethora of restaurants already thriving, this newcomer quickly established itself as a player. CBS Television City is nearby, contributing diners from the media and music set, who often throng the bar area. Curving ceiling-to-floor picture windows and concrete floors impart an appropriate sense of urban chic.

American comfort foods (burgers, pasta, chicken salad) baby the professionally addled, while a generous selection of domestic and European cheeses, an impressive variety of Italian and Spanish charcuterie, as well as vegetarian dishes suit sophisticated palates. All appreciate the reasonable prices, efficient service, and oh-so-hip vibe. BLD is open for breakfast, lunch and dinner—hence the name.

BOA

011

8462 W. Sunset Blvd. (at La Cienega Blvd.)

Phone: 323-650-8383
Web: www.boasteak.com
Prices: **$$$**

Lunch & dinner daily

This is not your grandfather's steakhouse. For starters, tiny BOA is on the Sunset Strip, inside the swanky Grafton Hotel. And its high-dollar, ultra-modern design, incorporating padded ultrasuede walls and an organic "sculpture" of sandblasted driftwood, is a far cry from the clubby classic.

Happily, BOA reveres doing things right, beginning with polite and careful service, and extending to impeccably prepared salads—applewood-smoked bacon, Maytag blue cheese, and buttermilk ranch dressing in the Cobb, for instance—and a "Turf" menu hewing to tradition with a bone-in Kansas City filet mignon and a 40-day dry-aged New York strip. The burgers are not your grand-dad's either; bet he never had one with Kobe beef and black-truffle shavings.

Café des Artistes

012

1534 N. Mc Cadden Pl. (at Sunset Blvd.)

Phone: 323-469-7300
Web: www.cafedesartistes.info
Prices: **$$**

Mon – Fri lunch & dinner
Sat – Sun dinner only

In this bungalow-cum-French bistro, on a street chockablock with studio buildings, sound stages and post-production houses, the buzzing in the dining room and pretty courtyard comes from a lot of "below-the-line" folks who actually *make* movies—the editors, technicians and craftspeople whose names account for most of the credit roll.

The décor is a bright mélange of paintings and antiques. *Les créations culinaires* are classic bistro fare, like onion soup *gratinée*, pâté with cornichons, and grilled spicy merguez sausage. Jean Renoir and François Truffaut would find the "Main Courses Avec Les Frites"—the steamed mussels, the steak tartare prepared tableside, the filet with peppercorns and *sauce flambée Cognac*—as familiar as an old Arriflex.

Campanile

013

Mediterranean XXX

624 S. La Brea Ave. (bet. W. 6th St. & Wilshire Blvd.)

Phone: 323-938-1447 Mon – Sat lunch & dinner
Web: www.campanilerestaurant.com Sun lunch only
Prices: $$$$

Charlie Chaplin put up the building, but lost it in a divorce the year Wall Street ended its divorce from reality, taking the Jazz Age down with it. What remains is that Chaplinesque determination to get it right every time. That spirit defines Campanile: the immaculate décor, the proficient service, the terrific food.

Credit chef Mark Peel, who debuted Campanile in 1989, with entrées (fillet of seared rare pompano on a bed of sliced cucumber and avocado) that are deft and surprising. Assorted breads hail from the ovens of Peel's La Brea Bakery next door.

Chaplin wanted you to laugh. Campanile wants you to smile, raise a glass of wine, and grapple with the challenging task of choosing among tarts, cakes, puddings and cheeses for dessert.

Carlitos Gardel

014

Argentinian XX

7963 Melrose Ave. (bet. Crescent Heights Blvd. & Fairfax Ave.)

Phone: 323-655-0891 Mon – Fri lunch & dinner
Web: www.carlitosgardel.com Sat – Sun dinner only
Prices: $$

Stars, including Lauren Bacall not long ago, used to speak fondly of dining on Santa Monica's stretch of Montana Avenue the way they do today about Melrose Avenue's run east from Beverly Hills. Stars frequent Carlitos Gardel too, their chummy photos with the owner decorating the masculine. old-fashioned dining room.

Named for Carlos Gardel (ca.1890-1935), the still-revered King of Tango, the restaurant features the *parrillada mixta*, or mixed grill, so popular in Argentina. Here that can mean short ribs, grilled skirt steak, sweetbreads, chorizo, and black sausage finished at your table on a small grill. All else on the menu revolves around meat, about which—to borrow the title of one of Gardel's films, *La Casa es Seria*— the house is serious.

Celadon

Fusion

015

7910 W. 3rd. St. (at Fairfax Ave.)

Phone: 323-658-8028
Web: www.celadongalerie.com
Prices: **$$**

Tue – Sun dinner only

An alternative to eateries at the Farmers' Market, which it faces, this Asian-minimalist culinary gallery behind a striking façade of translucent panels offers an innovative range of well-matched Asian-French marriages united under soft lighting by an attentive staff. Opened in late 2006, Celadon draws an *au courant* clientele.

On any given day, you might find hamachi citrus salad with ponzu gelée, Kumamoto oyster jalapeño, Ahi tuna with foie gras and braised daikon, spicy Szechwan noodles, or whole steamed halibut with ginger and sesame sharing the stage with a side of truffle-scented herbs. A full separate bar offers a variety of sake and cocktails. Desserts like black-sesame custard with a brulée of baby bananas sweetly evoke the Orient.

Chameau

Moroccan

016

399 N. Fairfax Ave. (bet. Beverly Blvd. & Oakwood Ave.)

Phone: 323-951-0039
Web: www.chameaurestaurant.com
Prices: **$$**

Tue – Sat dinner only

This French Moroccan restaurant forsakes the usual North African Casbah motif for a contemporary French-Arab look of vivid blue and red surfaces, modern furnishings and dramatic accent lighting. That it is discreetly tucked into the Fairfax district, known for its Orthodox Jewish community, is very LA—a city whose schools recognize more than 90 languages.

The menu changes with the seasons, but favorites like homemade bread, merguez sausage with grilled onions, and grilled skewered beef and lamb shank grace the selection year-round. Market-fresh daily fish specials are prepared Mediterranean-style. Traditional couscous courses run the gamut: vegetable, lamb, beef, sausage, game hen, fish. End your Moroccan respite with a Spanish Muscatel.

Chaya Brasserie

017

Fusion

8741 Alden Dr. (bet. Georges Burns Rd. & Robertson Blvd.)

Phone:	310-859-8833	Lunch & dinner daily
Web:	www.thechaya.com	
Prices:	$$$	

In feudal Japan, a *chaya* was a roadhouse where travelers found rest, a meal and a pot of tea. For more than 20 years in this high-end shopping district, loyals have filled the bar, the stylish dining room, the interior bamboo garden and the flowered patio into the late-night hours. The draw? Top-notch fusion fare in a space filled with flowing fabrics and Asian objets d'art—and live jazz on Sundays.

The menu changes, but defers to fans of special sushi rolls like the Banzai—spiced soft-shell crab with sprouted radish seeds and cucumber—while offering seductive pasta, fish and meat entrées (lobster ravioli; miso-marinated sea bass; hot and cold paella with chicken and saffron). This brasserie is as locally secure as the one in Paris called Lipp.

Dakota

018

American

7000 Hollywood Blvd. (at Orange Ave.)

Phone:	323-769-8888	Dinner daily
Web:	www.dakota-restaurant.com	
Prices:	$$$	

Housed within the Roosevelt Hotel across from Grauman's Chinese Theatre is an enclave of brown suede armchairs, leather-topped tables, and warm-toned wood paneling. With its Spanish Renaissance exterior and supper-club atmosphere inside, the Dakota is a rare find in this touristy part of Hollywood, attracting a mixed crowd of casual diners who favor designer jeans over suits and ties.

Though the restaurant describes itself as a steakhouse, Dakota reaches well beyond typical steakhouse fare with a diverse selection of expertly prepared entrées. A wonderfully composed dish of tender, bacon-wrapped pork shoulder plated with buttery soft polenta and earthy, wilted Swiss chard epitomizes the slow-food style of cooking espoused by this kitchen.

Hollywood

Dolce Enoteca

Italian 🍴

019

8284 Melrose Ave. (at Sweetzer Ave.)

Phone: 323-852-7174
Web: www.dolcegroup.com
Prices: $$$

Dinner daily

With its sienna plaster exterior and long, awning-covered walkway (seemingly designed for grand entrances and flashing paparazzi cameras), Dolce Enoteca asserts a commanding presence. Expect votive candles, banquettes and cushioned black leather chairs; an enclosed covered patio, separated from the main room by a clear glass wall, offers additional seating.

The menu skips through Italy from Risotti of the Earth (in Forest, Garden or Sea versions) to bowls of hearty pasta (think lobster demilunes with saffron-infused Champagne cream) to hearty osso buco Milanese—Dolce's signature dish.

The Dolce Group's celebrity backing insures a nightclub energy; come evening, the young and the restless gather here for loud music and creative cocktails.

Doug Arango's

American 🍴

020

8826 Melrose Ave. (at Robertson Blvd.)

Phone: 310-278-3684
Web: www.dougarangos.com
Prices: $$$

Mon — Fri lunch & dinner
Sat dinner only

As this guide was going to press, this gracious West Hollywood bistro was closing for a redesign. It's scheduled to reopen in September 2007 as Melrose Bar & Grill, with a new casual décor and a menu where no item is priced above $25. Melrose Bar & Grill will have the same owners and the same chef.

Although new dishes will be added to the menu, the crispy thin-crust pizzas and other comfort-food favorites (like the cedar-brined Berkshire pork chop served with house-cured sauerkraut) are slated to be retained. Daily chalkboard specials, affable service and a wine list strong in California labels round out the dining experience here.

Hollywood

Dusty's

021

Contemporary ✗

3200 W. Sunset Blvd. (at Descanso Dr.)

Phone:	323-906-1018	Lunch & dinner daily
Web:	www.dustysbistro.com	
Prices:	$$	

Opened by a Québécoise several years ago, this chic little bistro quickly became a Silver Lake hit, a phenomenon encouraged by the generous portions. Locals crowd in for breakfast omelets, crêpes and French toast. Lunch features organic salad, grilled French sandwiches and burgers of lamb, turkey, crab, and Black Angus beef. French influences flavor dinner entrées such as duck sautéed in a Merlot sauce, and a goat-cheese-crusted, thyme-infused rack of lamb. Among the hearty sides is *poutine*, Quebec's famed snack: fries covered with mozzarella curds and gravy.

Spare and swanky by turns—a ruler-straight row of tables, a swoopy banquette—the interior reflects the enthusiasm that revitalized this area, home to early motion-picture studios.

eat. on sunset

022

Contemporary ✗✗

1448 N. Gower Ave. (at Sunset Blvd.)

Phone:	323-461-8800	Tue – Fri lunch & dinner
Web:	www.patinagroup.com	Sat dinner only
Prices:	$$$	Mon lunch only

This stylish brick house represents the Patina Group's makeover of its former Pinot Hollywood. The restaurant has a restful air, drawing locals with its serious cooking and reasonable prices. On the patio, olive trees and vine-laced walls create a bit of serenity. Couches under the stars and inside add a homey feel to cocktail parties. The dining room is made luminous by an atrium ceiling and warmed by a fireplace when it's cool outside.

American favorites fill the bill in the form of hamburgers, meatloaf, and macaroni and cheese, along with salads, sandwiches, and salmon (the latter slow-baked to preserve the delicate texture within, served over leeks and garnished with crispy onion rings). The kitchen is open late on Friday and Saturday.

Hollywood

The Foundry on Melrose

C o n t e m p o r a r y

023

7445 Melrose Ave. (at Gardner St.)

Phone:	323-651-0915	Tue – Sat dinner only
Web:	www.thefoundryonmelrose.com	
Prices:	**$$$**	

Eric Greenspan learned from El Bulli disciplines in Spain, worked for Alain Ducasse in New York and at Patina in Los Angeles, and put it all together here, tapas-style, in a swanky setting featuring live jazz some nights and DJ music others.

The tasting menu retraces the chef's culinary odyssey with dishes like poached albacore tuna and chanterelle mushrooms in a chile sauce, and tenderloin in asparagus purée, coupled with wines from small vineyards in France and California.

The Moderne curve of the yellow, black-ribbed bar, the dining room's leather chairs and banquettes, and Pop Art canvases suit the culinary sophistication. A gorgeous terrace, with a fireplace and a graceful olive tree, appeals to the stylish, entertainment-industry crowd.

Geisha House

J a p a n e s e

024

6633 Hollywood Blvd. (at Cherokee St.)

Phone:	232-460-6300	Dinner daily
Web:	www.geishahousehollywood.com	
Prices:	**$$$**	

Where else but in Hollywood, where anything can be a movie set, would you find this sexual fantasy of a restaurant? Perfumed with incense and exploding on your senses from the moment you enter, Geisha House envelops you in red. A red tower of stacked fireplaces rises toward the ceiling, lending its flickering glow to the downstairs dining room and the mezzanine above.

While there's much to distract you (even the waitresses are eye-candy), don't ignore the share-able dishes that fill the menu with everything from sushi, hand rolls and robata-yaki to the delicious miso-marinated black cod—a house specialty.

Kimono-clad geishas roam the floor, while the twenty-something crowd sports designer jeans and includes an A-list of Hollywood hotties.

Girasole

Italian ✗

025

225 1/2 N. Larchmont Blvd. (bet. Beverly Blvd. & 3rd St.)

Phone:	323-464-6978	Wed – Fri lunch & dinner
Web:	N/A	Tue & Sat dinner only
Prices:	$$	

Girasole has no liquor license, but when did you last find a restaurant that doesn't charge for corkage? You'll find it here, in this small, unpretentious, family-owned spot in Larchmont Village. The commercial heart of the Hancock Park district will bring to mind a vintage downtown in a small Midwestern city.

From the *cucina Italiana* come appetizers like grilled and marinated vegetables, a score of pasta dishes, and a dozen classic *secondi*—osso buco, turkey or veal scallopini, stews of veal and lamb. Minestrone is available year-round; pumpkin dumplings with butter and sage are seasonal.

The motif inside is meant to suggest Venice. A quartet of tables on the sidewalk terrace is a lovely place to sit and sip an after-dinner espresso.

Hollywood

Grace

Contemporary ✗✗✗

026

7360 Beverly Blvd. (at Fuller Ave.)

Phone:	323-934-4400	Tue – Sun dinner only
Web:	www.gracerestaurant.com	
Prices:	$$$$	

Chef/partner Neal Fraser commanded several prominent kitchens before he decided to grace Hollywood with this venture. The chef's range serves his ambition, producing the likes of North Sea cod cheeks in a sauce perfumed by shiso, pan-fried John Dory in a saffron reduction, and memorable sweets (think crispy peach galette with bourbon brown-sugar ice cream). His multicourse tasting immerses diners in innovative American cuisine. Come on Burger Night (Sunday) for a classic made with dry-aged Highland beef and your choice of buttermilk, blue, gruyère or truffle cheese.

"Grace" suits Michael Berman's sophisticated design, which creates an imposing wine display and an elegant lounge where a mix of trend-setters and business executives hold sway.

Hatfield's

027

7458 Beverly Blvd. (bet. Gardner & Vista Sts.)

Phone:	323-935-2977	Mon – Sat dinner only
Web:	www.hatfieldsrestaurant.com	
Prices:	**$$$**	

Quinn and Karen Hatfield ended a transcontinental odyssey after raves in San Francisco and New York by opening this little jewel evoking California's iconic early-20th-century Craftsman style.

Like the genre—concrete floor, white walls, small tables elegantly dressed—their approach looks simple: a boutique wine list salutes France and Italy, while a short menu honors seasonal markets. But appetizers such as charred Japanese octopus, friseé and smoked-trout salad, and sautéed foie gras reveal their ambition. With entrées like pan-roasted New Zealand snapper, wild King salmon steamed in cabbage, and a Long Island duck breast done up with exotic mushrooms, butternut squash and a whisky-prune smear, it's clear that the Hatfields are going places.

Hirozen

028

8385 Beverly Blvd. (at Orlando Ave.)

Phone:	323-652-0470	Mon – Fri lunch & dinner
Web:	www.hirozen.com	Sat lunch only
Prices:	**$$**	

If gastropubs existed in Japan, Hirozen would qualify with its lively ambience, laid-back clientele and superior fresh raw fish. This Spartan 30-seat space (plus 8 seats at the sushi bar) in a banal strip mall delivers creatively prepared, moderately priced fare served with genuine friendliness.

What's fresh daily at local markets determines the changing selections. That makes for luxuriously tasty sushi items (one bite and it's *sayonara* for most) of abalone, striped bass and red snapper. The house tuna burger (sans bun) is seared medium rare and laced with aromatic herbs. A choice of quality sake nicely complements hot entrées like Kobe-style beef *tataki* (meat seared outside but left raw in the middle) and shrimp-filled zucchini-flower tempura.

The Hungry Cat

Seafood

029

1535 N. Vine St. (at Sunset Blvd.)

Phone: 323-462-2155   Tue – Fri & Sun lunch & dinner
Web: www.thehungrycat.com   Mon & Sat dinner only
Prices: $$

On the street level of the Sunset and Vine business-residential complex (a milestone symbol of Old Hollywood's continuing revival), this friendly spot takes its menu cues from traditional East Coast raw bars and has fans purring with delight. The thoroughly modern industrial-chic room accommodates 50, including seats at a comfortable zinc bar fronting the open kitchen. A heated back patio makes room for 25 more.

There are oysters and littleneck clams on the half shell, of course, along with "peel 'n eat" shrimp, Dungeness crab cakes, lobster rolls, house-smoked salmon and American sturgeon and paddlefish caviar. For those wishing to stay ashore, there's the Pug Burger, a comforter topped with bacon, avocado and blue cheese.

Il Capriccio on Vermont

Italian

030

1757 N. Vermont Ave. (bet. Kingswell & Melbourne Aves.)

Phone: 323-662-5900   Mon – Fri lunch & dinner
Web: www.ilcapriccioonvermont.com   Sat – Sun dinner only
Prices:

Rustic Italian dishes reign here, made of the freshest ingredients and served in copious portions. The food is traditional, featuring trattoria recipes the owners claim date back to the Renaissance—al dente pasta dishes with strong, aromatic flavors, polenta, *frutti di mare*. The atmosphere is casual, the prices most affordable, and the staff will welcome you as if you were already a regular.

With its tinted Tuscany-style walls hung with regional paintings, the dining room lies within view of the open kitchen. Large rows of wooden tables, dressed with white linen and brown butcher paper, are most appealing at night under soft lighting. Best place for lunch? On the heated sidewalk patio, where you can feel the neighborhood's bohemian vibe.

Hollywood

Il Sole

031

8741 Sunset Blvd. (at Sherbourne Dr.)

Phone:	310-657-1182	Dinner daily
Web:	N/A	
Prices:	**$$$**	

Celebrity sightings compete with the food at this little Sunset charmer, where the fare is Old World Italian with California accents, and paintings and pottery evoke the Old Country. Hollywood players frequent the house, where salads, pasta, soups, roasted fish, chicken and risotto number among the usual suspects.

Il Sole teems with buzz, so if a sauce lacks pizzazz, or a pastry is dry, no one seems to care (wafer-thin starlets don't really come to eat, after all)—though they do enjoy perusing the Italian, French and Californian labels that fill the wine list. The prices are up there, but no one seems to care about that either.

Small tables nuzzle close together, so rubbing shoulders with a Show Business Someone is often not just a metaphor.

Ita-Cho

032

7311 Beverly Blvd. (bet. Fuller Ave. & Poinsettia Pl.)

Phone:	323-938-9009	Tue – Sat dinner only
Web:	N/A	
Prices:		

Its interior may suggest an industrial cafeteria, but Ita-Cho delivers satisfying home cooking, good service and exceptional value. Located on bustling Beverly Boulevard, next door to the well-known Angelini Trattoria, it offers an inviting assortment of sashimi (but not sushi) along with teriyaki, vegetarian dishes (tofu, eggplant, broccoli), broiled, baked and deep-fried fish (black cod, green mussels, eel, octopus, squid), soups (mushroom, clam, miso) and lovely salads, all nicely presented. Sakes come hot and cold.

The crowd is a pleasant mix of young and old, known and unknown. If you're pressed for time, avoid the busy evening hours between seven and nine, when you're most likely to have to wait in line for a seat in the boisterous room.

Jar

033

Contemporary 🍴

8225 Beverly Blvd. (at Harper Ave.)

Phone: 323-655-6566
Web: www.thejar.com
Prices: $$$

Mon – Sat dinner only
Sun lunch & dinner

A discreet sign marks this self-proclaimed chophouse *(not steakhouse)*, where chef Suzanne Tracht revives "retro dishes from the American culinary repertoire" including her signature pot roast and Kansas City steak. Swanky 1970s décor—curved paneled walls, flying-saucer light fixtures, a leather banquette, velvet chairs—evoke the last decade when you could eat this way without feeling guilty.

So go ahead—dig into those purple yams with crème fraîche and chives. Or go Monday for the mozzarella menu, which offers more than a dozen presentations. On Sundays, brunch surprises with lobster benedict and corn pancakes.

The service is courteous and the crowd urban but not flashy, if a bit on the noisy side after eight at night when Jar is packed.

Katana

034

Japanese 🍴

8439 W. Sunset Blvd. (at La Cienega Blvd.)

Phone: 323-650-8585
Web: www.katanarobata.com
Prices: $$

Dinner daily

Celebrities turn out at Katana in droves, but they don't upstage the extensive list of innovative sushi, particularly the specialty rolls like pale pink toro with jalapeño strips, or the skewers of grilled meats and vegetables coming off the robata bar's open-flame grills (the robata grill area can get smoky; you may want to sit at the sushi bar instead). The chefs know how to make a simple miso soup sing with flavor, and how to fill hand-rolled *temaki* cones of thin soy paper with delectable stuff, say shredded crab meat, or a spicy mix of minced yellowtail, chile paste, scallions and sesame oil.

The light is dim, the noise level high in this Zen-den-meets-nightclub. A lovely outdoor patio overlooking Sunset Boulevard is SRO on warm evenings.

Koi

035

730 N. La Cienega Blvd. (at Melrose Blvd.)

Phone: 310-659-9449   Dinner daily
Web: www.koirestaurant.com
Prices: $$$

Rock and movie stars and the people who orbit them celebrate themselves in this stylish establishment, where black floors, an earth-toned palette with red accents, polished wood and the flickering light from scores of small white candles honor Asian aesthetic traditions in a contemporary form.

The same attention is given to the preparation of signature dishes like the baked crab hand roll with crispy rice. There's innovation here—California rolls with baked scallops or sautéed shrimp, tuna tartare on crispy wontons, Kobe beef carpaccio with fried shiitakes and a yuzu citrus sauce. Sake comes "by the bamboo" or the bottle; brands are described by taste.

Pulsing club music, security bouncers and paparazzi out front foster the private-club vibe.

La Boheme

036

Contemporary

8400 Santa Monica Blvd. (at Orlando Ave.)

Phone: 323-848-2360   Dinner daily
Web: www.globaldiningca.com
Prices: $$$

Named for the Puccini opera, La Boheme serves food that sings with high-quality ingredients, both local and seasonal. On any given day, simple pastas include rich and earthy mixtures (say roasted mushrooms and brown butter sauce, a chestnut ravioli, a Maine lobster risotto with corn purée), while main courses run from seared wild salmon to an aged sirloin strip steak. Unusual desserts share Italian touches and full-voiced sweetness.

In keeping with the restaurant's bohemian spirit, the dressy-casual crowd reflects West Hollywood's indie-film community. There are two dinner seatings, and their popularity makes reservations a must. This spacious production closed for a few months in summer 2007 to undergo a significant facelift.

La Terza

Italian ✗✗

037

8384 W. 3rd St. (at Orlando Ave.)

Phone:	323-782-8384	Lunch & dinner daily
Web:	N/A	
Prices:	**$$**	

At 23, owner Gino Angelini was the youngest chef in an upscale hotel restaurant in his native Italy, where he cooked for presidents (Mitterand, Gorbachev) and popes (John Paul II). *La Terza* ("third" in Italian) is his latest LA venture, and it's *primo* in many Angelenos' hearts.

His bi-level space has an open wood-burning rotisserie and grill where most of the meats, including wild boar, squab, duck, lamb and beef, are prepared. Portions are small (actresses in LA don't eat much), strongly flavored and well-executed from high-quality, often imported ingredients. Most of the specials trace their heritage to Italy's Piemonte and Emilia-Romagna regions, but nearly every province is represented in the interesting selection of Italian varietals.

Le Clafoutis

French ✗✗

038

8630 Sunset Blvd. (at Sunset Plaza Dr.)

Phone:	310-659-5233	Lunch & dinner daily
Web:	N/A	
Prices:	**$$**	

The fancy boutiques and eateries squeezed into Sunset Plaza are the unofficial city hall of the Sunset Strip, where stars shop, dine and don Frisbee-sized sunglasses to frustrate the paparazzi. Named for a custardy French pastry traditionally studded with cherries (but not necessarily found on the dessert cart here), this well-run, morning-to-midnight brasserie is both a scene and a fine place to enjoy dishes with French flair. The sunny canopied sidewalk patio is a great place for lunchtime people-watching.

Simple preparation is the rule, and the staff happily fulfills special requests for fickle Angelenos. Much-ordered favorites include the crab cake, and the smoked-salmon and goat-cheese roulade. Pastries, *naturellement*, are stellar.

Le Petit Bistro

French ☓

039

631 N. La Cienega Blvd. (at Melrose Ave.)

Phone:	310-289-9797	Mon – Fri lunch & dinner
Web:	www.lepetitbistro.us	Sat – Sun dinner only
Prices:	$$	

Surrounded by hip eateries and a hot nightclub, this old-fashioned Paris-style bistro seems out of time and place, and so offers a refreshing respite. The narrow dining room is usually crowded. The décor is bistro basic, with a burgundy banquette, vintage liquor ads, butcher-paper-covered tables, and waiters dressed in *garçon de café* garb.

Escargots, onion soup *gratinée*, mussels cooked with white wine and shallots, roasted chicken with herbs de Provence, and grilled ribeye with *pommes frites* constitute traditionally Gallic fare, while California-style grilled fish and salads cater to those with more health-conscious tastes. Desserts include classic profiteroles and a buttery bread pudding. Portions are honest, tasty and moderately priced.

Le Petit Greek

Greek ☓

040

127 N. Larchmont Blvd. (bet. Beverly Blvd. & 1st St.)

Phone:	323-464-5160	Lunch & dinner daily
Web:	www.lepetitgreek.com	
Prices:	$$	

It's not surprising that the food, décor and music here are authentic, for the Houndalas family was in the restaurant business in Greece for generations before setting up shop in Larchmont Village in 1988. In a little house, complete with a sidewalk patio, the green and white dining room is decorated with Old Country photos and bottles of wine from around the world—including, of course, a wonderful collection of Greek labels.

The signature baby rack of lamb shares menu space with an abundance of Mediterranean salads, dips, moussaka, kebobs and pasta dishes. Unpretentious and affordable, with casual yet efficient service and generous portions, Le Petit Greek is a refreshing alternative to LA's often trendy and pricey restaurant scene.

The Little Door

Mediterranean XX

8164 W. 3rd St. (bet. Crescent Heights Blvd. & La Jolla Ave.)

Phone: 323-951-1210   Dinner daily
Web: www.thelittledoor.com
Prices: $$$

What's behind the Little Door? It's worth your while to find out. Once inside, you'll step into a garden patio overflowing with bright flowers, ferns and lush greenery. By day, sunlight filters in through the open skylight; after dark, the stars twinkle overhead in the night sky. In back you'll discover the open-air winter garden, its sparkling blue and white color scheme conjuring up the Mediterranean.

Hip, moneyed Beverly Hills denizens who frequent this place have no qualms about shelling out big bucks for the wine and food. The menu summons each season with premium ingredients and generous portions of pasta, small plates and daily specials.

Check out The Little Next Door for breakfast and lunch, or gourmet goodies to go.

Locanda Veneta

Italian X

8638 W. 3rd St. (bet. Robertson & San Vicente Blvds.)

Phone: 310-274-1893   Mon – Fri lunch & dinner
Web: www.locandaveneta.com   Sat – Sun dinner only
Prices: $$

This enchanting trattoria across the street from Cedars-Sinai Hospital has claimed a following since it first opened in 1998, which may explain why its trademark red banquettes are a bit the worse for wear. Tiny tables make room for only 50 diners.

Authentic food translates into old friends like *vongole* soup (clams steamed in tomato broth); bruschetta with porcini; spinach and ricotta gnocchi; or a hearty ragù of shredded filet mignon, wild mushrooms and Marsala. Specials are chalked on a blackboard behind the bar. The dining room is sunny during the day, dimly candlelit for dinner. For more intimacy, ask for a table by the window or on the covered outdoor terrace.

Next door, the 3rd Stop Café, operated by the same owners, offers less expensive fare.

Lucques

043

Mediterranean

8474 Melrose Ave. (at La Cienega Blvd.)

Phone:	323-655-6277	Tue – Sat lunch & dinner
Web:	www.lucques.com	Sun – Mon dinner only
Prices:	$$	

In this brick building, once the carriage house of silent-screen star Harold Lloyd, chef Suzanne Goin salutes Alice Waters' practice: a short seasonal menu featuring the best organic produce. Her Mediterranean palette has a French flair (Lucques is a variety of olive grown in southern France and Italy).

A grilled whole fish served at lunch with roasted nectarines, couscous and pistachio *aillade* (a kind of aïoli) may be reprised at dinner in the company of black rice, sizzling ginger, kumquats and sambal. Seductive combinations please diners with the likes of warm duck confit with figs, dandelion, walnuts and dates, or a ricotta semifreddo with berries and hibiscus syrup.

If you have time, explore the street's oh-so-upscale antique shops.

Madeo

044

Italian

8997 Beverly Blvd. (bet. Doheny Dr. & Robertson Blvd.)

Phone:	310-859-4903	Mon – Fri lunch & dinner
Web:	N/A	Sat – Sun dinner only
Prices:	$$$	

Though surrounded by the trendiest of furniture shops, Madeo remains anti-trend in the best possible way. The Italian-speaking brothers and their Tuscan kinfolk who staff Madeo offer Italian hospitality with a matching décor of vintage wood beams, immaculate table linens, and a large, circular bar where guests can relax in comfort.

First-timers and regulars, a mix of Italian-born Angelenos and Hollywood A-listers, are all treated like friends here. On the plate, they savor generous portions skillfully prepared, and entrées like veal Milanese, *gamberini griglia* (grilled langoustines brushed with olive oil and garlic), linguini with pesto, and a choice of vegetable, mushroom or seafood risotto. No one seems to blink at the high prices.

Hollywood

Marino

045

Italian

6001 Melrose Ave. (at Wilcox Ave.)

Phone:	323-466-8812	Mon – Fri lunch & dinner
Web:	N/A	Sat dinner only
Prices:	$$$	

If you're in the mood for something traditional and romantic, rather than avant-garde, this family-run restaurant is a fine choice. The calm atmosphere, old-fashioned décor (eclectic Italian paintings and antiques), intimate lighting and polite, efficient service seem to have all been in place here for decades.

Upon entering, patrons are immediately tempted by a glass-fronted armoire displaying antipasti—meats, aged cheeses, marinated olives and vegetables. If you order the branzino, a whole fish cooked en *papillote*, Marino's owner may do the honors himself, deboning the fish at your table before dressing it with olive oil and pepper, then presenting it with a creamy asparagus risotto.

The solid wine list finds strength in Italian vintages.

M Café de Chaya

046

Californian

7119 Melrose Ave. (at la Brea Ave.)

Phone:	310-278-0588	Lunch & dinner daily
Web:	www.mcafedechaya.com	
Prices:		

Sequestered in a tiny strip on Melrose at La Brea (around the corner from Pink's Hot Dogs), this cafe is the most casual of the family of restaurants that started with Chaya Brasserie in Beverly Hills.

Quintessentially Californian, made-to-order salads (tuna tataki topped with greens and fresh avocado) share the menu with rice bowls, hot and cold sandwiches, and wraps. Avoiding refined sugars, dairy products, red meat and poultry, the cafe uses tempeh "bacon" in its California club, and thinly sliced grilled seitan (wheat gluten) in its Carolina-style barbecue.

They do a brisk carry-out business for customers who can't find a seat among the handful of tables inside and out on the sidewalk (where traffic noise can interrupt conversation).

Mimosa

Hollywood

047

8009 Beverly Blvd. (bet. Edinburgh & Laurel Aves.)

Phone:	323-655-8895	Mon – Sat dinner only
Web:	www.mimosarestaurant.com	
Prices:	$$	

LA isn't known for convincing French bistros, but this one has the feel. Edith Piaf's voice rains from the stereo in a room crowded with red banquettes, cramped tables, and black-and-white photographs of Paris. Of course, there's a sidewalk terrace, and much of the staff are *Français*.

Owner Jean-Pierre Bosc's motto is: "No truffles, no caviar, no bizarre concoctions." Fittingly, each meal begins with humble jars of cornichons and spicy olives, served simply with bread and butter. French comfort food includes a generous choice of charcuterie, whole roast chicken *grand-mère*, cassoulet, and skate *Grenobloise* with hazelnut butter, capers and lemon confit.

Adding to bistro verisimilitude are desserts like chocolate mousse and pear financier.

Mirabelle

048

8768 Sunset Blvd. (bet. Horn Ave. & Sherbourne Dr.)

Phone:	310-659-6022	Lunch & dinner daily
Web:	www.mirabellehollywood.com	
Prices:	$$	

Run by the Germanides family since 1971, Mirabelle has evolved, decade by decade, from what was originally a hamburger stand to a chic and stylish maturity. Today, diners may choose the sheltered patio, with its rotating rooftop, copper-top bar, rattan seating and tropical greenery—ideal for an afternoon martini or a glass of wine under the stars—or the more formal dining area, where classic paintings hang above inviting booths.

Gallic touches are evident in the excellent sauces and provincial dishes like roast chicken breast with a creamy Dijon mustard sauce, with herb-infused polenta and, *naturellement*, French fries. The portions are large, the service attentive, the prices reasonable, and the kitchen is open after midnight on busy nights.

Nishimura

049

Japanese

8684 Melrose Ave. (at San Vicente Blvd.)

Phone:	310-659-4770	Mon – Fri lunch & dinner
Web:	N/A	Sat dinner only
Prices:	$$$	

 It's easy to miss this modest ivy-covered bungalow, across the street from the Pacific Design Center. Once you spot the number on the façade, you'll note there's no entrance on the street side. To find the door, discreetly hidden behind a high wood fence, you'll have to walk through a little courtyard garden.

Once inside the bright little dining room, with its sushi bar and smattering of tables, you'll be treated to a selection of sushi and sashimi, along with thin-sliced (hamachi with Serrano chile, dai-dai sauce and cilantro) and seared dishes (kanpachi with ginger, grated garlic and yuzu pepper sauce). Depending on what's in season, specials add local seafood such as grilled Santa Barbara shrimp.

Expect gracious service and high prices.

Nyala Ethiopian

050

Ethiopian

1076 S. Fairfax Ave. (bet. Olympic Blvd. & Witworth Dr.)

Phone:	323-936-5916	Lunch & dinner daily
Web:	www.nyala-la.com	
Prices:		

 This family-owned enterprise is said to be the best in LA's Little Ethiopia. Behind a modest storefront façade, a small dining room decorated with African artifacts attracts a boisterous bunch for combination platters of chicken, lamb or beef, as well as seafood and vegetarian dishes. The cuisine is authentic, flavorful and reasonably priced.

Pleasantly sour pancake-like bread known as *injera*, ubiquitous in Ethiopia, is a staple here too. The spongy crêpes of teff flour serve as both platter and utensil; tear off a piece and pinch your fingers to pick up portions, or use the bread to soak up the various aromatic sauces. In addition to Ethiopian wine, you can quench your thirst with strong coffee, hot spiced tea or African beer.

Hollywood

Off Vine

Californian ☓☓

051

6263 Leland Way (at Vine St.)

Phone:	323-962-1900	Lunch & dinner daily
Web:	www.offvine.com	
Prices:	**$$**	

A jewel in a not-quite-yet gentrified neighborhood, this lovingly restored century-old artifact of the Arts and Crafts Movement is a serene oasis amid Old Hollywood's trafficky streets. There are two cozy dining rooms, but the place to be is on the front porch, extended by a beautiful garden terrace. Come evening, if the weather is warm, this can be a very romantic place.

Pasta dishes, including vegetarian choices, are plentiful, and the familiar salads—Cobb, Caesar and Niçoise—are hearty. Picnic baskets, available in summer and favored by those bound for performances at the Hollywood Bowl, feature tasty items like cold poached salmon or pecan-breaded chicken cutlets with pear rosemary sauce. Call it comfort food with a European touch.

Pastis

French ☓

053

8114 Beverly Blvd. (at Crescent Heights Blvd.)

Phone:	323-655-8822	Dinner daily
Web:	www.lapastis.com	
Prices:	**$$$**	

LA's Pastis (no relation to the boisterous bistro in Manhattan's Meatpacking District) welcomes guests into a tiny, candlelit interior, where bare farm tables, framed mirrors and vintage photos of the French countryside are juxtaposed with the sounds of club music—a distinctly LA twist.

Charcuterie, pâté, and *coq au vin* bespeak the traditional, while bouillabaisse, mussels *marinière*, and a lovely lavender crème brulée add Provençal accents. On Wednesdays, buy a bottle of wine and get a complimentary bottle to take home. (Alas, you can't drink it here.)

For a splurge, indulge in the five-course pairing menu. In this feast, the chef matches up imported wines with dishes like lobster bisque, roasted monkfish and walnut-crust strawberry tart.

Ortolan ❀

French ✕✕✕

8338 W. 3rd St. (bet. Orlando & Sweetzer Aves.)

Phone:	323-653-3300	Tue – Sat dinner only
Web:	www.ortolanrestaurant.com	
Prices:	$$$$	

Lane Taylor/Ortolan

Hollywood

An opulent cream-colored cocoon lit by crystal chandeliers, Ortolan excels at being posh. In the monochromatic dining room, leather banquettes nestle against walls swathed in creamy drapes. The adjacent slate-gray lounge area holds a wall of planters filled with edible herbs.

Chef Christophe Emé's personality infuses his inventive presentations. An amuse-bouche of asparagus soup may be served in a test tube, while fish keeps warm on hot stones. Settle in for the evening with the chef's ten-course tasting, or order à la carte from the *menu plaisir*. Pleasure will indeed be yours as you tuck into such dishes as a perfectly roasted fillet of John Dory, its mild flavor balanced by ravioli filled with ricotta and spicy chorizo.

Ortolan takes its name from a small European songbird, a member of the bunting family, once prized by gourmands (it's now illegal to hunt these birds).

Appetizers
- English Pea "Cannelloni" with Asparagus and Mushroom Carpaccio
- Macaron of Foie Gras Confit with Truffle
- Langoustines with Basil, Chickpea and Shot of Minestrone

Entrées
- Lamb Pastilla, Rosemary White Beans, Tomato Confit, Mint Salad
- Sea Bass, Spinach Cannelloni, Bone Marrow, Swiss Chard

Desserts
- Chocolate - Soufflé Tart, Passionfruit, Milk Emulsion
- Apple - Panna Cotta, Caramel Ice Cream, Apple Confit
- Citrus - Orange, Lemon, Grapefruit Sorbet, Meringue

Pizzeria Mozza

054

Hollywood

641 N. Highland Ave. (at Melrose Ave.)

Phone:	323-297-0101	Lunch & dinner daily
Web:	www.mozza-la.com	
Prices:	$$	

When Mozza, a joint venture by Mario Batali and Nancy Silverton, opened in late 2006, it was one of the most sought-after lunch tables in town. You'll still spot celebrities aplenty at this boisterous trattoria, where round wood tables crowd together and hundreds of bottles of reasonably priced Italian wines are displayed at the two large open bars.

Every day brings a new special. The antipasti are house originals, surprises like green asparagus in a grain-mustard sauce with almonds and caponata, and roasted corn with green-garlic butter. Pizzas have thin crusts, and toppings run from prosciutto, tomato and mozzarella to littleneck clams.

Little sister, Osteria Mozza, with an entrance off Melrose around the corner, opened in summer 2007.

Republic

Contemporary

056

650 N. La Cienega Blvd. (at Melrose Ave.)

Phone:	310-360-7070	Mon – Sat dinner only
Web:	www.therepublicla.com	
Prices:	$$$	

A new kid on the block, Republic is already known for its glamorous ambience and hip lounge, officially declared a "hot" spot. You pass a shimmering waterfall at the entrance before entering the soaring, semi-circular dining room. If you favor alfresco dining (and smoking) head for the patio, with its cabanas and retractable ceiling.

You'll remember the 20-foot-high glass-enclosed wine wall of horizontally stacked bottles, retrieved by acrobatic servers using a system of cables and harnesses. The first-class wine list cites labels from around the world.

Film-industry players and celebrities come here to see and be seen—especially on weekends—while they nosh on Maine lobster corndog appetizers, then dig into steaks fired on a mesquite grill.

Providence ❀

Seafood 🍴🍴🍴

5955 Melrose Ave. (at Cole Ave.)

Phone:	323-460-4170	Sat – Thu dinner only
Web:	www.providencela.com	Fri lunch & dinner
Prices:	$$$$	

Jeff Oshiro/Providence

Hollywood

While it doesn't require divine aid to find Providence, you will need to look carefully for this unmarked, two-story building, tucked amid the shops on a stretch of Melrose that's a bit removed from the buzz. The soaring dining room is contemporary in décor; the small patio is more intimate, paved with stone, lit by flickering candles, and covered by a tented roof. Guests include everyone from movie producers to a lively mix of locals.

Chef and co-owner Michael Cimarusti's menu dotes on beautiful, seasonal arrangements of fish and shellfish, but accommodates meat lovers too. Ambitious creations range from the innovative (striped bass with fennel purée, green-lip mussels, cockles and kumquats) to the experimental (roasted squid and pig's ear with piquillo chile peppers, olive paste and almonds). When the kitchen hits it right, the food here is nothing less than heavenly.

Appetizers	*Entrées*	*Desserts*
• Dungeness Crab Napoleon, Mango, Pickled Red Jalapeño	• Diver Scallops with Sugar Snaps and Chanterelles	• Chocolate Cremeux with Raspberry Gelée and Lambic Espuma
• Santa Barbara Spot Prawns, Fennel Purée, Purple Basil	• Tai Snapper with Sweet Corn, Chili-Lime Syrup and Maitakes	• Coconut Panna Cotta with Carrot Sorbet
• Lobster Bloody Mary, Horseradish Crème Fraîche, Celery-Vodka	• Soft Shell Crab, Piquillo Pepper Purée	• Concord Grape Sorbet, Brioche Crumbs, and Peanut Butter Powder

SIMON L.A.

Contemporary ✗✗

057

8555 Beverly Blvd. (at La Cienega Blvd.)

Phone: 310-278-5444

Lunch & dinner daily

Web: www.sofitella.com

Prices: $$$

Chef Kerry Simon's crowd-pleaser in the hip Sofitel *(see hotel listing)* suggests a high-end coffeeshop with its curved booths, open kitchen and devotion to American comfort food—but a coffeeshop for Beautiful People who want *his* hamburger and thick-cut fries, and *his* oven-warm chocolate cookies.

Simon's serious about dishes some sniff at, say meatloaf or shrimp cocktail (served with horseradish purée). You dip his fried Gulf shrimp in a ponzu sauce, or go lightly with a beef tartare and seared carpaccio duo. Taste is paramount, as in a ribeye piled with cipollini onions, or a seared sea bass over couscous. For dessert, Simon says try the Junk Food Sampler, a retro assortment of childhood favorites.

On nice days the outdoor patio is dreamy.

Social Hollywood

Mediterranean ✗✗✗

058

6525 W. Sunset Blvd. (at Hudson Ave.)

Phone: 323-462-5222

Dinner daily

Web: www.socialhollywood.com

Prices: $$$$

Leave it to Jeffrey Chodorow to turn the former Hollywood Athletic Club into LA's next go-to restaurant. Designed c.1922 by the architects who did Grauman's Chinese Theatre, this Art Deco landmark once served as a gym and entertainment venue for the likes of Charlie Chaplin and Cecil B. DeMille. Today, with help from designer Mark Zeff, Chodorow has fashioned a 28,000-square-foot playground comprising bars and dining rooms, private screening rooms, and a members-only lounge called Level II.

In the ground-floor Moroccan Room, cuisine roams from Turks and Caicos conch to a short-rib tagine cooked in a spicy-sweet Oaxacan mole. Stained-glass lanterns cast a sultry glow on the vaulted ceilings, restored to reveal their original frescoes.

Sona

401 N. La Cienega Blvd. (bet. Beverly Blvd. & Melrose Ave.)

Phone:	310-659-7708 Tue – Sat dinner only
Web:	www.sonarestaurant.com
Prices:	$$$$

Mark Takahashi/Sona

Hollywood

David and Michelle Myers' creation, nestled in a small white house at the corner of La Cienega and Westmount, bespeaks a passion for excellence, attention to detail and meticulous technique.

Six- and nine-course dégustation menus offer a memorable start-to-finish experience. Or you can go it alone, selecting "Firsts" like superbly fresh white asparagus, dressed with black-truffle-infused vinaigrette and a stripe of stinging-nettle purée. "Seconds" roam from silky, caramel poached salmon to a Nebraska beef tenderloin that needs no knife. The wine list cites more than 2,200 bottles of the finest European and domestic labels, including rare vintages such as a 1929 Massandra pink Muscat from Russia.

Amazing desserts (think buttermilk waffle served with a warm apple compote and pear honey sorbet) come from Boule Atelier a few blocks away, run by David's wife, Michelle.

Appetizers
- Maine Lobster Risotto, Kaffir Lime Emulsion
- Marinated Peekytoe, Seaweed Jelly, Yuzu Marmalade
- Bigeye Tuna, Swiss Chard with Lime Pickle, Fresh Green Almonds

Entrées
- Shortribs, Glazed Daikon, Celery Root and Shiso Salad
- Macadamia-crusted Hawaiian Opah, Spicy Pineapple
- "Kazuzuki" Liberty Farms Duck, Blood Orange and Fennel

Desserts
- Peach Tart, Juniper Ice Cream, Oatmeal Stout Foam
- Sona S'mores- Marshmallow, Graham Cracker, Chocolate Sorbet

Sonora Café

Hollywood

180 S. La Brea Ave. (bet. Beverly Blvd. & 3rd St.)

Phone:	323-857-1800	Tue – Fri lunch & dinner
Web:	www.sonoracafe.com	Sat – Sun dinner only
Prices:	$$	

This warehouse conceals an appealing space of high, exposed-beam ceilings, with an open bar, an inviting lounge area warmed by a fireplace, and a comfortable dining room of banquettes and well-spaced tables. Southwestern-style chandeliers add a rustic elegance.
Portions are generous, the flavors are fresh, strong and spicy. Blue-corn enchiladas are stuffed with chicken and served with a smoky sauce of poblano chilies and tomatillos. A trio of quesadillas brings brie, leeks with goat cheese, and lobster crème fraîche. The likes of jumbo shrimp *a la plancha* shares the menu with Sonora's signature dish, Texas barbecue pork chops with sweet-potato purée, tamales and mango papaya salsa.
Traffic noise can be distracting on the small terrace.

Surya

8048 W. 3rd St. (bet. Crescent Heights Blvd. & Laurel Ave.)

Phone:	323-653-5151	Tue – Fri lunch & dinner
Web:	N/A	Sat – Mon dinner only
Prices:	$$	

Named after the Hindu sun god, this contemporary restaurant sits on one of the most pleasant blocks of Third Street. Red walls hung with photos of Indian landmarks are offset by the black ceiling and blond wood floors.
Crisp *samosas* (pastry shells with savory fillings) make a good place to start. They come with a pair of aromatic mint and tamarind dipping sauces. Tandoori (chicken, lamb, turkey, prawns) dishes, curries and vegetarian choices are served with freshly baked naan and saffron-infused basmati rice.
Chef/owner Sheel Joshi is half English, which may explain desserts like bread pudding with marmalade, and saffron rice pudding. To drink, there's a Euro-American wine list, or *lassi,* a non-alcoholic yogurt drink served sweet or salted.

Sushi Roku

Japanese

8445 W. 3rd St. (bet. Croft Ave. & La Cienega Blvd.)

Phone:	323-655-6767	Mon – Sat lunch & dinner
Web:	www.sushiroku.com	Sun dinner only
Prices:	**$$$**	

Don't be dissuaded by Sushi Roku's brick town-house exterior or the fact that it's part of a small chain. This is one of the most popular sushi spots in town. The décor of gray concrete, bamboo and stone suits a fashionista crowd, who are served by a courteous waitstaff in black kimonos.

The fare is delectable, with an emphasis on fish. Innovative Cal-Asian dishes include black cod in sweet miso, Chilean sea bass with yuzu butter, King crab croquettes, and seared albacore with crispy wontons. Sushi reigns here, presented according to the market's best each day. For the chef's choicest selections, go for the *omakase* sampling, which will give you a comprehensive experience. For dessert, try the decidedly un-Japanese vanilla profiteroles.

Table 8

Californian

7661 Melrose Ave. (at Spaulding Ave.)

Phone:	323-782-8258	Mon – Sat dinner only
Web:	www.table8la.com	
Prices:	**$$$**	

Depending on your mood, the décor of this current hotspot may seem romantic and sexy or sinister. Black tents cover the façade and float above the pavement. The opulent all-black bar-and-lounge area leads to a dining room clad in dark leather and mohair walls, black-varnished tables and a purple chandelier, with a waitstaff all dressed in—you guessed it—black.

Imaginative and elegantly presented dishes follow the California credo of seasonal cuisine. Thus sturgeon wrapped in pancetta might share the bill with duck breast and squash blossoms, pompano with sunchokes and black-truffle crêpes, or grilled Kobe beef served with a shiitake-mushroom tart. For smaller appetites there's a menu of light fare in the lounge (where no reservations are needed).

Hollywood

Talésai

Thai XX

064

9043 Sunset Blvd. (at Doheny Dr.)

Phone: 310-275-9724
Web: www.talesai.com
Prices: $$

Mon – Fri lunch & dinner
Sat – Sun dinner only

Upscale, elegant, welcoming and unpretentious, this may be the best Thai experience in town. (Not to mention that this stretch of Sunset holds some of LA's top pop-music venues.) Superior ingredients and top-notch preparation distinguish the delicately seasoned dishes, which include Thai curries, cashew chicken, classic pad Thai, crispy duck, spicy unagi, sea bass tamarind, and Thai dim sum, to name a few. Vegetarians are taken care of here with selections ranging from spicy eggplant with Thai basil and black-bean sauce to Eight Princes, eight types of Asian vegetables sautéed with light soy sauce. Oh, and then there's the excellent martini list.

For more casual fare, visit the Cafe Talésai in Beverly Hills *(9198 Olympic Bvd.)*.

Taste

Contemporary X

065

8454 Melrose Ave.
(Bet. Orlando Ave. & La Cienega Blvd.)

Phone: 323-852-6888
Web: www.ilovetaste.com
Prices: $$

Lunch & dinner daily

Snug in a Spanish Colonial-style bungalow next door to Lucques, this casual spot has a raised, covered sidewalk terrace and a cozy pair of double-sided dining rooms filled with dark leather walls and bistro-style banquettes.

The simple, tasty food reflects the best traits of the Golden State cuisine: mostly light, chockful of vegetables, ideal for alfresco dining. Lunch specials feature a ravioli of the day along with gourmet sandwiches and salads. At dinner the menu expands to include the likes of red-wine-braised short ribs, curried chicken or Cajun shrimp. Thin and crispy pear tartine, and chocolate parfait devil's-food cake are the signature desserts.

After lunch, poke around in the high-end antique shops that abound on nearby blocks.

Tower Bar

Californian

066

8358 Sunset Blvd.
(bet. Crescent Heights Blvd. & La Cienega Blvd.)

Phone:	323-654-7100	Dinner daily
Web:	www.sunsettowerhotel.com	
Prices:	**$$$**	

This Moderne building once hosted Howard Hughes, John Wayne, Benjamin "Bugsy" Siegel and other Tinseltown players. Beyond the lounge, the curving walnut-paneled dining room, jazz pianist, and old-school maitre d' evoke the era when stars bound for Europe booked passage on the *Normandie*.

The fashionable clientele reflects the West Hollywood upscale gay scene and the anything-goes mainstream movie world, so dress accordingly. Chef Dakota Weiss specializes in skillfully prepared Californian fare with a French-Italian twist. Starters include raw shellfish or shaved fennel; for entrées, consider a lobster Cobb Salad, roasted lamb T-bone, or an organic omelet with black truffles and caviar. For the city-wide views, request a window table.

Vert

Contemporary

067

6801 Hollywood Blvd. (at Highland Ave.)

Phone:	323-491-1300	Lunch & dinner daily
Web:	www.wolfgangpuck.com	
Prices:	**$$**	

On the fourth floor of the Hollywood & Highland complex (next door to the Kodak Theatre), this colorful Wolfgang Puck venue mixes cusines styles from an Italian trattoria, a French brasserie and an American restaurant, all with an Asian accent. Portions are ample and the dishes well executed, if not always Oscar-worthy.

Proscuitto pizza, Cobb and Niçoise salads, and *soupe a l'oignon* share the bill with prime cheeseburgers, sashimi, roasted organic chicken breast, and orecchiette with shrimp and fresh tomatoes. Complimentary bread baskets hold an interesting assortment served with goat cheese scented by fruity olive oil.

Of the complex's three eateries, Vert is the most affordable, with validated parking in the building's lot.

Vivoli Café

068

7994 Sunset Blvd. (at Laurel Ave.)

Phone:	323-656-5050
Web:	www.vivolicafe.com
Prices:	

Lunch & dinner daily

Cached away in a strip mall on Sunset, Vivoli is no longer a secret. The menu in this busy little place features authentic and simple dishes from every region of the Italian boot, complemented by daily chef's specials like homemade lasagna with ragù and béchamel. Osso buco is a signature here, along with thin-crust pizzas and favorite starters like calamari *fritti*, lightly fried and served with a lemony *arrabiata* sauce spiked with hot peppers, garlic and herbs. A marinara sauce with capers and olives finishes the branzino *alla Livornese.*

The décor is unassuming but warm, with yellow walls and wine bottles on display. Portions are generous, prices affordable, and the Italian-speaking staff sets a friendly tone of relaxed hospitality.

WA

069

1106 N. La Cienega Blvd. (at Holloway Dr.)

Phone:	310-854-7285
Web:	N/A
Prices:	$$

Tue – Sun dinner only

Don't let the adjoining 7-Eleven dissuade you. WA's two tiny rooms, with their linen-draped tables and large picture windows, are masters' workshops. Here three Matsuhisa-schooled chefs dazzle you with dishes such as shrimp sushi prepared in two courses—bodies first, then crispy deep-fried shells—grilled Chilean sea bass with eggplant and optional foie gras, and King crab served with beurre blanc. Presentation is noteworthy and the service is smooth.

The menu is color-coded for cold, hot and lightly cooked courses, and the sake list is divided into dry, full-bodied and light varietals. To taste the chefs' work at the top of their art, consider the *omakase* menu; it's pricey but worth it.

An added bonus: there's free parking in the mall's garage.

Xiomara on Melrose

Latin American

6101 Melrose Ave. (at Seward St.)

Phone:	323-461-0601	Sun – Fri lunch & dinner
Web:	www.xiomararestaurant.com	Sat dinner only
Prices:	$$	

This is the third location for celebrated chef Xiomara Ardolina, a native Cuban whose creative and refreshing take on Latin flavors has consistently won raves from critics and diners alike. The upscale vintage décor, with a beautiful old wooden bar, wrought-iron staircase, and framed mirrors, is offset by white linens, candlelight and a mix of soft jazz and Cuban music engendering a romantic mood.

Consider the charcuterie platter, a bevy of Spanish cured sausages, plus *dulce de membrillo* (quince paste) and Manchego cheese. A spicy, crusted lamb shank comes with a casserole of *malanga* (a root vegetable) and mojo, while saffron rice and twice-fried plaintains accompany tasty *nuevo cubano* chicken *patacones*. Mojitos are practically obligatory.

Yabu

Californian

521 N. La Cienega Blvd. (bet. Melrose & Rosewood Aves.)

Phone:	310-854-0400	Mon – Sat lunch & dinner
Web:	N/A	Sun dinner only
Prices:	$$	

Yabu's small, one-story, wood-and-concrete house offers a large menu including a changing board of daily specials prepared by affable sushi chefs whose enthusiasm induces shouted progress reports on your order. Exposed ceiling beams add rustic warmth to the immaculate sushi bar and sunny dining room. The serene outdoor bamboo garden and brick fireplace banish the West Hollywood bustle. Only the servers hustle here.

Chefs prepare traditional wheat udon and buckwheat soba noodles as you watch, along with assorted sushi chosen for freshness. There is tempura, made thin and light for dishes like *ten don* (shrimp and vegetables over steamed rice), and *yakimono*, in which marinated meats are skewered and then grilled or broiled.

The only parking is on the street.

Hollywood

Pasadena

Located less than 10 miles (via the Pasadena Freeway) from Downtown Los Angeles, Pasadena seems a world away from the bustle and sprawl of its neighbor to the southwest. The San Gabriel Mountains loom over this sunny city of 146,000, whose 22.5 square miles captured the nation's fancy long ago as proof of what California living could be.

Originally part of the vast lands encompassed by San Gabriel Mission—California's fourth—the area that would become Pasadena passed through several different owners as Mexican-era grant lands in the late 1800s. This acreage eventually came into Anglo-American hands, incorporating as the city of Pasadena in 1886.

In 1890, the city's elite Valley Hunt Club marked New Year's Day with a procession of flower-bedecked horses and carriages. The event quickly evolved into an annual tradition, now known as the **Rose Parade** *(right)*.

A GENTEEL PAST

Pasadena became a winter resort for wealthy Easterners, whose homes account for scores of buildings listed on the National Register of Historic Places. None surpass the Italian Renaissance **Tournament of Roses House** *(391 S. Orange Grove Blvd.)*, now the event's headquarters.

Pasadena's 23 parks impart a bucolic air, and there's a sense of time long past in the **Old**

Pasadena Historic Area. This quarter holds some 200 buildings from the late 1800s, including the Gamble House, a masterpiece of the American Arts & Crafts Movement. In the district's 22 blocks you'll find much of the city's best dining, entertainment and nightlife.

California's official State Theater, **The Pasadena Playhouse** *(39 S. El Molino Ave.)*, is famed for its stellar casts. The **Rose Bowl Stadium**, home of the New Year's Day football classic, hosts the Southland's premiere flea market on the second Sunday of every month.

RENOIR, ROSES AND ROCKETS

Cultural offerings are ripe for the picking here. The **Norton Simon Museum** exhibits masterpieces from one of the world's choicest private art collections. In nearby San Marino, treasures at the **Huntington Library** include rare books and manuscripts as well as a world-class collection of 18th- and 19th-century British art. The Huntington's Botanical Gardens nurture 15,000 plants from all over the world.

As for the local brain trust, faculty and alumni (including Albert Einstein) of the **California Institute of Technology** have won 31 Nobel Prizes. For fans of space exploration, NASA's **Jet Propulsion Laboratory** *(4800 Oak Grove Dr.)* hosts free tours once a week (advance reservations required).

Long Photography / Pasadena CVB

Arroyo Chop House

Steakhouse

001

536 S. Arroyo Pkwy. (bet. E. Bellevue Dr. & Pico St.)

Phone: 626-577-7463   Dinner daily
Web: www.arroyochophouse.com
Prices: $$$$

With its white-linen tablecloths, wooden chairs and dark slat blinds, the contemporary Craftsman interior of this ivied chophouse is classic Main Street, evoking scenes in film where pols knife into prime beef and each other as they decide how democratic things will be. The servers are attentive and affable, and a traditional paneled partition topped with etched glass sets most tables and booths apart from the chatter at the bar's leather stools.

A steakhouse-sized wedge of chilled heart of iceberg lettuce is topped with a creamy yet subtle blue-cheese dressing; a filet mignon is served with béarnaise sauce and a side of sugar-snap peas. It's all-American and it's serious food, backed by piano music softly playing under the conversation.

Bistro 45

Californian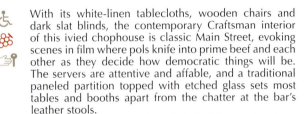

002

45 S. Mentor Ave. (bet. Colorado Blvd. & Green St.)

Phone: 626-795-2478   Tue – Fri lunch & dinner
Web: www.bistro45.com   Sat – Sun dinner only
Prices: $$

Three intimate dining rooms huddle inside this vintage Art Deco building, its little front garden scented by lavender and rosemary. The smartly casual interior and swanky red bar and lounge—even the sheltered patio— create a residential serenity bolstered by the welcoming staff.

Pure Golden State, the menu spotlights fresh produce, organic meats, farm-raised duck and Pacific seafood. Regional favorites include wild-caught fried calamari served with spicy mustard sauce for dipping, or perhaps a Pacific pink grouper prepared bouillabaisse-style, paired with shellfish in a lobster broth. As for wine, a large selection of California Pinot Noir and Cabernet Sauvignon is first up at bat, with red Bordeaux ready in the bullpen.

Bistro 561

003

Californian

561 E. Green St. (at Madison Ave.)

Phone:	626-405-1561	Mon – Fri lunch & dinner
Web:	www.561restaurant.com	
Prices:	$$$	

This bistro is staffed entirely by students (with supervision) completing their training at the California School of Culinary Arts. The subdued sage-green tones and exposed brick walls, made bright and airy by large windows, are tastefully simple. Not so simple is the goal of blending classic French techniques with the Asian and Mediterranean influences of Southern California cuisine.

It can work like this: a whole artichoke heart is sliced in half and grilled, then presented with a seasoned mint purée. Or a vibrant saffron risotto is topped with pieces of snow-white Maine lobster and a cotton-candy-pink foam whipped from blood oranges.

Call in advance for reservations; this popular place occasionally closes for school holidays and private parties.

Celestino

004

Italian

141 S. Lake Ave. (bet. Cordova & Green Sts.)

Phone:	626-795-4006	Mon – Fri lunch & dinner
Web:	www.calogerodrago.com	Sat dinner only
Prices:	$$	

This outpost of the Drago empire, located on lively Lake Avenue, offers authentic regional Italian fare. Sit on the front patio if you want to take in the scene, or opt for a table in the rustic dining room, with its sunny walls and open kitchen. The attentive brigade is uniformed in white aprons and black bow ties.

Italian recipes favor the North, with classics like roasted rabbit with black olives, osso buco *alla Milanese* (with saffron risotto), and lasagne bolognese (with meat ragù). A salad of Belgian endive, seasoned with blue cheese, tosses walnuts, apple and radicchio together. You'll wait 15 to 20 minutes for the risotto of the day, but the delay is worth it.

Desserts include standards like tiramisú and panna cotta.

Derek's

California

005

181 E. Glenarm St. (at Marengo Ave.)

Phone:	626-799-5252	Tue – Sat dinner only
Web:	www.dereks.com	
Prices:	$$$	

Greenery hides this cozy spot in the back of a little mall off the Arroyo Parkway, where courtyard trees engender a sense of bucolic escape. Inside, earthy floor tiles, dark-stained wood and burnt-sienna walls create a romantic ambience, while black-clad servers, white linens and quality tableware set an elegant tone.

European-schooled restaurateur Derek Dickenson maintains a fine local and international wine list, and oversees an ambitious seasonal menu supplemented by daily market selections. There's French technique here, as in a salad of cooked chilled slices of beet, topped with balsamic-dressed frisée and garnished with a wedge of aged goat cheese; or roasted halibut garnished with beurre blanc. Rack of lamb Bordelaise is a menu mainstay.

Japon Bistro

Japanese

007

927 E. Colorado Blvd. (bet. Lake & Mentor Aves.)

Phone:	626-744-1751	Tue – Fri lunch & dinner
Web:	www.japonbistro-pasadena.com	Sat – Sun dinner only
Prices:	$$	Mon lunch only

If *Tokubetsu Junmai* means anything to you, you'll appreciate the fine sake selection here. That means rice wine matched with the dish, whether it's a combination sushi plate including delicacies like eel (*unagi*) and sea urchin (*uni*), or Japanese green peppers stuffed with spicy tuna, deep-fried tempura-style and finished with a sweet sauce.

Rice wines, like Western wines, are each uniquely suited to certain flavors, so servers will suggest a proper sake for a hot-spiced shrimp tempura or a beef or chicken teriyaki. Match the right rice wine with *chawan mushi*, a blend of seafood and vegetables baked in a soft silky custard, and you'll understand the art of sake pairing. There is validated parking nearby on Mentor Street, across from the Ice House comedy club.

The Dining Room at the Ritz-Carlton ✿

Pasadena

006

Contemporary ✖✖✖✖

1401 S. Oak Knoll Ave. (at Huntington Dr.)

Phone: 626-568-3900   Tue – Sat dinner only
Web: www.ritzcarlton.com
Prices: $$$$

The Ritz-Carlton, Huntington Hotel & Spa

Step onto the thick carpets of the clubby dining room at the Ritz-Carlton Huntington *(see hotel listing)* and you enter a serene cloister of Murano glass chandeliers, paneled walls, richly upholstered chairs and formal white china—what Old Southland Money prefers. This is a place where debutantes have debuted, exchanged marriage vows, and returned with their beloveds for milestone anniversaries since 1907.

Changing menus—including a multicourse tasting—balance meat and fish; all are expertly prepared and beautiful to behold. Accents are straightforward: a whisper of mint perfumes a lovely amuse-bouche of pea soup garnished with smoked salmon, while sautéed turbot on a bed of spaghetti squash, accompanied by mussels in a subtle curry broth, makes a delectable entrée.

Starry nights encourage alfresco dining on the garden terrace—just one more place to put on the Ritz.

Appetizers

● Tuna with Lentils, Micro Greens, Asian Vinaigrette and Spicy Mayonnaise

● Diver Scallops and Foie Gras with Kumquats and Jerusalem Artichoke Purée

Entrées

● King Salmon with Spinach, Preserved Lemon and Pickled Watermelon

● Merguez-spiced Lamb Chop and Loin with Melted Tomato Ratatouille

Desserts

● Chocolate Banana Croustillant with Rum Raisin Ice Cream

● Poached Pear in Warm Financier with Honey Thyme Ice Cream

Maison Akira

French 🍴🍴🍴

008

713 E. Green St. (at Oak Knoll Ave.)

Phone:	626-796-9501	Tue – Fri & Sun lunch & dinner
Web:	www.maisonakira.com	Sat dinner only
Prices:	$$$	

After studying with Joël Robuchon, chef/owner Akira Hirose worked at Maxim's in Paris and mastered the art of pastry at l'École de Lenôtre (as the tempting array of goodies in the display case at the entrance attest). His menu presents classic French cuisine accented by the flavors of his native Japan. Japanese touches come and go, as in a miso-marinated Chilean sea bass. Closer to the French fold is a duck and green-peppercorn pâté. A bow to Nippon, Akira's Bento box (also available as a Hollywood Bowl picnic takeout) is a popular lunch option.

The *maison* is high Gallic, with mustard walls, Impressionist paintings, flower-filled vases, high-backed Napoleonic chairs, and a tall fireplace. The famed Pasadena Playhouse is right around the corner.

Parkway Grill

California 🍴🍴🍴

009

510 S. Arroyo Pkwy. (at California Blvd.)

Phone:	626-795-1001	Mon – Fri lunch & dinner
Web:	www.theparkwaygrill.com	Sat – Sun dinner only
Prices:	$$$	

In a stand-alone redbrick building, with exposed ceiling beams and track lights above, and dark wood paneling, stained-glass panels and cushioned chairs below, Parkway Grill boasts archetypal contemporary West Coast design: warm, spacious, solid and comfortable.

The kitchen draws some of its spices, greens and garnishes from the garden out back, and whips up creations like a crab cake soufflé presented atop a creamy avocado purée, or a grilled Pacific salmon atop a purée of cauliflower and garnished with sautéed slices of wild mushroom and crisp sugar-snap peas. The wine list is long, as is the comfy bar.

Wearing white shirts and black ties, well-trained servers lend an air of relaxed professional confidence that puts the room at ease.

The Raymond

C a l i f o r n i a n

010

1250 S. Fair Oaks Ave. (at Columbia St.)

Phone:	626-441-3136	Tue – Sun lunch & dinner
Web:	www.theraymond.com	
Prices:	**$$**	

The Raymond Hotel closed in 1931, but its caretaker's cottage survives amid flowering bushes and trees secluding a brick patio dining area with umbrella-shaded tables and comfy chairs. The elegant décor inside the three small dining rooms compliments the building's Craftsman architecture.

Cuisine here relies on seasonal, locally grown produce. Thus a tomato and eggplant Napoleon—a chilled tower of disks of tender grilled eggplant, tomato slices and soft creamy mozzarella—is market fresh. California's burgeoning culinary vocabulary is spoken fluently here, as in a grilled, whole, boneless breast of skin-on chicken topped with a salsa of diced mango, papaya, pineapple, sweet peppers, red onion and cilantro.

Come for afternoon tea on weekends.

Saladang Song

011

T h a i

383 S. Fair Oaks Ave. (bet. California & Del Mar Aves.)

Phone:	626-793-5200	Lunch & dinner daily
Web:	N/A	
Prices:	💰💰	

This restaurant became so popular that the owners opened a second next door (*song* means "two" in Thai). The modern concrete and steel space with its lovely patio doesn't compete for attention with traditional fare like *Miang goong* (ground grilled shrimp flavored with lime, peanut and ginger) and a range of flavorful noodle dishes. Carnivores will appreciate the skewers threaded with generous portions of beef balls or marinated pork.

The outdoor terrace seems especially suited for Thai breakfasts (a choice of porridges) and the modestly priced lunch options. Seasonal dishes are updated regularly. If you want the hot stuff, look for specials like spicy seafood curry, after which your palate can be soothed with creamy, sweet Thai iced tea.

750 ml

012

966 Mission St. (at Meridian Ave.)

Phone:	626-799-0711	Dinner daily
Web:	www.750-ml.com	
Prices:	**$$$**	

Casual and charming, this new wine bistro in sleepy South Pasadena makes a great addition to the neighborhood. The restaurant sits across the street from the Gold Line metro station, so you can see the trains racing by from the large bay windows in the industrial-chic dining room.

Thoughtful touches abound: brown paper covers the linen-topped tables to catch spills; linen kitchen dishcloths serve as napkins. The menu changes daily to headline a handful of appetizers and main courses (roasted duck breast on a bed of sautéed leeks and celeriac purée), and a couple of rustic desserts (puff pastry with Asian pears in a pool of lavender-infused cream).

A two-sided sheet cites the selection of artisan wines, available by the bottle and the glass.

Shiro

013

1505 Mission St. (at Fair Oaks Ave.)

Phone:	626-799-4774	Wed – Sun dinner only
Web:	www.restaurantshiro.com	
Prices:	**$$$**	

Does French cuisine plus Japanese influences equal modern Californian? In chef/owner Hideo Yamashiro's spacious, pleasant and popular "South Pas" venue it does. The décor is simple and the setting economy-class, but what comes from the open kitchen is well made.

The fusion *Californie-Japonaise* produces appetizers like tuna sashimi with shaved parmesan and arugula, pan-fried oysters with a Champagne curry sauce, foie gras sautéed on pineapple with Port wine sauce, or asparagus tips with a vibrantly flavored fresh tarragon dressing, pecans and tomatoes. Entrées exhibit the same tasty melding of cuisines: a whole catfish (a house specialty) garnished with ginger, cilantro and a ponzu-soy sauce.

Free parking is available in the adjoining bank lot.

Trattoria Tre Venezie ✽

014

Italian ✗✗

119 W. Green St. (bet. S. Pasadena & S. De Lacey Aves.)

Phone:	626-795-4455	Tue – Thu & Sat – Sun lunch & dinner
Web:	N/A	Fri lunch only
Prices:	**$$$**	

Rizzi Sciolis/Trattoria Tre Venezie

In what resembles a mountain cottage, this homey trattoria devotes itself to the cooking of *I Tre Venezie*, the three regions in northeastern Italy with historical ties to Venice. The small bar is chockablock with bottles, and more than 80 grappas are poured by the glass.

Intensely flavored preparations don't compromise on authenticity. Dishes here are not based on thick tomato sauces, olive oil and basil as they are elsewhere. Instead, unusual house-made pastas, such as Bellunese ravioli filled with a dense purée of roasted red beets and coated with brown butter, will leave you yearning for a trip to northern Italy. Only *Tre Venezie* history could produce a *baccala' mantecato*, wonderfully reincarnated here as thin ovals of grilled polenta topped with creamy whipped salt cod. A master at multitasking, chef Gianfranco Minuz makes pasta from ancient organic grains, acts as pastry chef, and produces his own liqueurs.

Appetizers
- Cjalsons with Ricotta; Sweet Spices, Cocoa, with Smoked Ricotta
- Baccala' mantecato; Salt Cod, Polenta, Vegetable Julienne
- Apple and Celery Salad with Pestolato Cheese

Entrées
- Lamb Ravioli with Sautéed Zucchini
- Daily Fish cooked in Garlic and Vinegar with Soft Polenta
- House Bollito Misto served with Green Sauce, Mostarda and Horseradish Sauce

Desserts
- Crema del Gondoliere
- Presnitz; Baked Pastry with Dried Fruit and Nuts
- Dolce Di Cioccolato; Chocolate Dessert Served with Vanilla Sauce

Yujean Kang's

C h i n e s e

015

67 N. Raymond Ave. (bet. Holly & Union Sts.)

Phone: 625-585-0855   Lunch & dinner daily
Web: N/A
Prices:

Pasadena

As the best-known Asian house in Pasadena's Old Town, Yujean Kang's deserves all its accolades. Named after its chef, this simply decorated favorite serves gourmet food on white tablecloths to a regular lunch and dinner crowd, for prices that belie the quality. Spacious round tables face the front windows, while banquette seating lines one wall.

The extensive menu offers an assortment of seafood dim sum served with mustard, chile, and soy sauces, and unusual things like mushroom soup garnished with tofu, and hot-and-sour soup seasoned with red peppers and vinegar.

Dishes are subtly seasoned, allowing the fresh ingredients in preparations like beef Szechwan-style, and polenta with shrimp and mushrooms to assert their natural flavors.

TIERCE MAJEURE

RESERVE DE LA COMTESSE
SECOND VIN DU CHÂTEAU
PICHON LONGUEVILLE COMTESSE DE LALANDE

CHATEAU PICHON LONGUEVILLE COMTESSE DE LALANDE
GRAND CRU CLASSÉ EN 1855 · PAUILLAC

CHATEAU BERNADOTTE
HAUT-MÉDOC

33250 Pauillac - France - Tel. 33 (0)5 56 59 19 40 - Fax. 33 (0)5 56 59 29 78

WWW.PICHON-LALANDE.COM

Santa Monica Bay
Malibu, Marina del Rey, Venice

Within its 8.3 square miles, bounded by Santa Monica Canyon, 26th Street, Montana and Centinela avenues, LA's **Venice** district and the Pacific Ocean, is a city of about 88,000 ranging from beach layabouts to film folk, with a lifestyle-oriented sensibility overall.

LIVING WELL BY DECREE

Commerce crowds main streets, but in City Hall, a Streamline Moderne gem dedicated in 1939 to "civic responsibility," quality-of-life issues prevail. In 1875 the city's developers offered "the Pacific Ocean, draped with a western sky of scarlet and gold... a frostless, bracing, warm, yet languid air, braided in and out with sunshine and odored with the breath of flowers... and the song of birds." They weren't exaggerating much. Year-round, locals idle in palmy **Palisades Park** on the city's ocean bluffs or on Santa Monica and Will Rogers state beaches below, and walk, jog or pedal the 22-mile South Bay Bicycle Trail.

Pedestrian-only **Third Street Promenade** between Wilshire and the Santa Monica Place mall on Broadway is chockablock with cinemas, restaurants and stores catering to current tastes. Fine hotels rise along **Ocean Avenue** from downtown to Pico Boulevard. **Main Street** south of Pico is lined with bistros, boutiques and galleries.

There's old-fashioned amusement-park fun on the 1909 **Santa Monica Pier** *(below)* where the Hippodrome shelters an antique carousel. At the other end of the sophistication spectrum is Southern California's largest art-gallery complex, Bergamot Station *(2525 Michigan Ave.)*, home to the **Santa Monica Museum of Art**.

A TOWN CALLED VENICE

Founded by tobacco tycoon Abbot Kinney in 1905, Venice featured canals, a 1,200-foot pleasure pier and an arcaded Main Street built in the Venetian style. Today, nearby **Ocean Front Walk** is a carnival of street artists, vendors and body builders pumping iron in the Muscle Beach weight pen. Many regard the restaurant, club and gallery scene along Abbot Kinney and Grand boulevards and Main Street as among the most avant-garde in the LA Basin.

©Mark Gibson

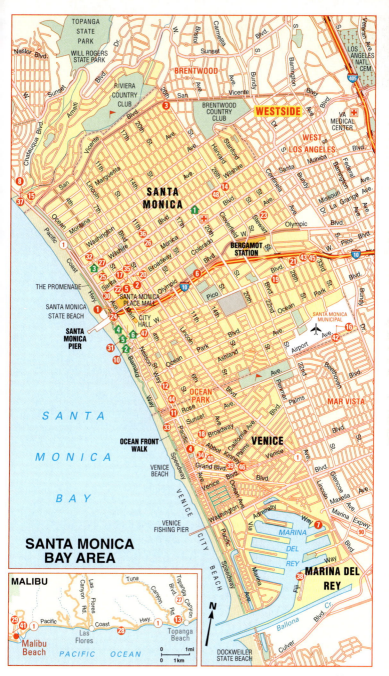

SANTA MONICA
BAY AREA

MALIBU

123

Abode

001

1541 Ocean Ave. (bet. Broadway & Colorado Ave.)

Phone: 310-394-3463   Lunch & dinner daily
Web: www.aboderestaurant.com
Prices: **$$**

One of the most promising new restaurants to open in LA in 2007, Abode is tucked back off Ocean Avenue in a little courtyard behind Il Fornio and Tengu (the valet stop is in front of Tengu). Bold dining-room décor says contemporary with dark slate walls, multi-toned wood floors, and elevated semi-circular leather banquettes.
Seasonal, sustainable and artisanal are the watchwords of this cuisine. The kitchen adds interesting twists to dishes like roasted duck breast enhanced with a tea-based broth incorporating hints of rooibos, pink peppercorns and chocolate. Unconventional desserts pull off daring flavor combinations, as in chocolate-ginger cake layered with silky chickpea cream.
That pleasant courtyard serves as a dining space on warm nights.

Akwa

Japanese

002

1413 5th St. (at Santa Monica Blvd.)

Phone: 310-656-9688   Mon – Sat dinner only
Web: www.akwarestaurant.com
Prices: **$$$**

Boldly colored stylish interiors and a seductive rooftop garden make it fun just to be here, if only for drinks and socializing, as many are. Innovative sushi and tasty Japanese cuisine reward those who stay to dine.
Innovative means creations like the Akwa shrimp tempura roll wrapped in toasted nori, topped with a mixture of tuna and crab spiced by chile and garlic, and drizzled with a smoky sauce of soy, eel extract and sweet rice wine. No Asian land can claim authorship of Jamaica Me Crazy, a roll of blackened Ahi tuna with fried plantains, cucumber and mango served with soy rice-wine vinegar and a chopped-scallion dipping sauce. A Wagyu Kobe burger served with truffle fries must qualify for some kind of world comfort-food title.

Amici

003

Italian 🍴🍴

2538 San Vicente Blvd. (at 26th St.)

Phone: 310-260-4900
Web: www.tamici.com
Prices: **$$**

Mon – Sat lunch & dinner
Sun dinner only

Brentwood is part of Los Angeles, but many within its putative boundaries consider it a separate city. So never mind that this charming trattoria bills itself as being in Brentwood, but is actually in Santa Monica. As some Malibu folks say, Brentwood is a state of mind. (The original Trattoria Amici is in Beverly Hills.)

The dining room is simple, yet stylish, with its Mexican tile floors, plank and beam ceilings, and surfeit of windows to suit the upscale, mostly local trade. The food is straightforward, generously served. You could easily make a meal out of a thick home-style cannellini bean and organic lentil soup alone, but the long list of pastas and the selection of meat, fish and pizza will please even the pickiest ladies who lunch.

Axe

004

Californian 🍴

1009 Abbot Kinney Blvd. (bet. Broadway & Brooks Ave.), Venice

Phone: 310-664-9787
Web: www.axerestaurant.com
Prices: **$$**

Tue – Sun lunch & dinner

The young, the socially conscious, and the free-spirited of Venice frequent Axe, whose name echoes a Yoruban salutation (pronounced ah-SHAY) that means "go with the power of the gods and goddesses."

Divine beings would no doubt count themselves blessed to feast on homemade breads, farm-fresh local produce and other organically grown foods that compose Axe's internationally influenced dishes. One day's lunch offered a Mediterranean albacore tuna salad with a lemon-cayenne vinaigrette, the fish smoked and served atop grilled artisan bread and spicy young arugula leaves crowned with buttery chickpeas, red onion slices and diced hard-boiled egg.

The atmosphere is no-frills and the feeling is communal, with sharing-size portions to match.

Santa Monica Bay

Border Grill

005

M e x i c a n XX

1445 4th St. (bet. Broadway & Santa Monica Blvd.)

Phone:	310-451-1655
Web:	www.bordergrill.com
Prices:	$$

Lunch & dinner daily

Tourists and young urban locals flock to this boisterous, bright and funky grill set on a tree-lined block near the Third Street Promenade shops and the Santa Monica Pier. Chefs Mary Sue Milliken and Susan Feniger, the "Two Hot Tamales" from the erstwhile Food Network TV show, have held sway at their flagship for more than 20 years.

Flavors speak boldly here, in well-composed *bocaditos* (small bites) and *platos especiales* (special plates), such as *carnitas Norteñas* (slow-braised pork, shredded and seasoned with garlic, chile and a hint of lime), that shine a spotlight on modern Mexican cuisine.

Be sure to make reservations, or be prepared to wait for a table. Parking options include a valet after 6pm and a parking garage across the street.

The Buffalo Club

006

A m e r i c a n XXX

1520 Olympic Blvd. (bet. 14th & 16th Sts.)

Phone:	310-450-8600
Web:	www.thebuffaloclub.com
Prices:	$$$$

Mon – Fri lunch & dinner
Sat dinner only

To the uninitiated, the industrial neighborhood, blank façade (look for the valet stand), and weathered neon "COCKTAILS" sign suggest a place you might enter with trepidation. Inside, however, Honduran mahogany paneling, antiqued mirrors and leather club chairs define an exclusive take on a vintage New York chophouse.

Industry types begin lunch here with oysters and caviar, then discuss their newest ventures over the likes of prime Angus New York steak with blue-cheese butter and Club fries, or country-fried chicken salad with pecans, cornbread croutons and ranch dressing. Dessert may just be the best part of a meal here, as evidenced by the rich and creamy vanilla-bean pudding set over a layer of tart red raspberries.

Cafe del Rey

Contemporary ✗✗

007

4451 Admiralty Way (near Promenade Way), Marina del Rey

Phone: 310-823-6395
Web: www.cafedelreymarina.com
Prices: **$$$**

Lunch & dinner daily

One of the best restaurants in the Marina Del Rey area, this cafe also enjoys one of the best locations hereabouts, overlooking some of the 7,000 hulls berthed in the world's largest man-made small-boat harbor. The interior architecture sports a 70s condo loft look, but most eyes are drawn to the pretty maritime panorama filling the windows.

Asian influences and American preferences fill the seasonal menu with sushi rolls of salmon, tuna, shrimp and eel; appetizers of pan-fried duck potstickers served on little beds of finely diced apple and cucumber; and a boar bacon-wrapped filet mignon. The availability of choice Hawaiian-caught fish, such as grouper, ono and blue snapper, flown into nearby LAX makes for interesting "day-boat" offerings.

Caffe Delfini

Italian ✗✗

008

147 W. Channel Rd. (at Pacific Coast Hwy.)

Phone: 310-459-8823
Web: N/A
Prices: **$$$**

Dinner daily

Across the street from trendy Giorgio Baldi, Caffe Delfini offers a more low-key option for Italian food. The cafe-style menu in this charming neighborhood spot features a short list of main courses, a long list of pastas, and nightly specials that typically star seafood. The skilled kitchen presents simple pleasures like a creamy rigatoni gorgonzola, and linguine *mare*, swimming with shellfish. Desserts are lush.

The shingled taupe exterior has an inviting beach-cottage look, while the cozy dining room is crowded with rattan chairs and small linen-covered tables with votive candles and decanters of vinegar and olive oil. Windows look out onto the sidewalk, and Italian music plays softly.

Valet parking is essential on this busy street.

Capo

Italian ✗✗

009

1810 Ocean Ave. (at Pico Blvd.)

Phone: 310-394-5550   Tue – Sat dinner only
Web: N/A
Prices: $$$$

In a cottage hiding just off the Ocean Avenue sidewalk in Santa Monica, Capo's cabin-like interior of wood floors, truss-plank ceiling and brick fireplace contrasts with the sophisticated décor—paintings, velvet drapes, European bistro chairs, backlit wooden wine cabinets, tabletop bud vases and flickering oil lamps—all *molto romantico*.

Excellent ingredients are the boss here, dictating that Italian courses be prepared simply, while producing bold flavors with a rustic technique. Zucchini blossoms stuffed with goat cheese are served with roasted tomatoes and garlic; large grilled shrimp come with a medley of lightly seasoned Tuscan beans. And after such lovely dishes, savor a tangy Meyer lemon semifreddo drizzled with blueberry compote.

Catch

Seafood ✗✗

010

1910 Ocean Way (at Pico Blvd.)

Phone: 310-581-7712   Lunch & dinner daily
Web: www.catchsantamonica.com
Prices: $$$

Airy as an ocean breeze, this recent addition to the Casa del Mar hotel *(see hotel listing)* combines a stunning location on the beach with a solid menu of delectable seafood. From the windows you can catch panoramas of the Pacific waves crashing on the white sand, but the best catch will be on your plate.

European technique is evident in the seafood entrées, as in a finely seasoned crispy skate wing entrée, caramelized and served on a bed of braised, vinegar-tangy savoy cabbage, the fish wearing a pesto-like strip of deep-green puréed herbs; or tender Gulf prawns atop bucatini pasta, accompanied by wild broccoli. Starters of sushi, sashimi and *crudo* are fashioned at the mother-of-pearl sushi bar. All in all, an impressive debut for this newcomer.

Chaya Venice

 International

110 Navy St. (at Main St.), Venice

Phone:	310-396-1179
Web:	www.thechaya.com
Prices:	$$$

Mon – Fri lunch & dinner
Sat – Sun dinner only

Life in Venice, or Venice Beach as some call it, blends laid-back lifestyles with intense careerism. Many residents work in the arts or entertainment, and are drawn to chef Shigefumi Tachibe's fusion of French and Japanese cuisine. Reflecting the area's casual style set on a foundation of determined discipline, Chaya makes for some of the neighborhood's best and most sophisticated dining.

Sushi-bar patrons may order from the full menu, which features international seafood determined by the market. International is the key word; Mexican spices fire up a Tuscan-style bean soup; a Californian arugula pesto tops grilled wild Canadian salmon. There is a good and generous selection of wines by the glass, and the bar is noted for creative mixology.

Chinois on Main

 Asian

2709 Main St. (at Hill St.)

Phone:	310-392-9025
Web:	www.wolfgangpuck.com
Prices:	$$$$

Wed – Fri lunch & dinner
Sat – Tue dinner only

Open for more than two decades now in Santa Monica, Wolfgang Puck's Chinois on Main fuses high-quality California products with classic cooking techniques. The resulting dishes (signatures include whole sizzling catfish, and Chinois chicken salad) are sized to share, and explode on your palate with expertly balanced flavors.

Asian shabby-chic describes the décor, which incorporates bamboo wainscoting, Asian artwork, two prominent peacock statues, and a large central skylight in a blend of Orient-meets-California-beach style. If you want a front-row seat for the culinary show, grab a chair at the counter that flanks the open kitchen.

Before or after a meal, meander the surrounding blocks and explore some of Santa Monica's artsy boutiques.

Cholada

013

Thai

18763 Pacific Coast Hwy. (near Topanga Beach Dr.), Malibu

Phone:	310-317-0025	Tue – Sun lunch & dinner
Web:	N/A	Mon dinner only
Prices:	☕☕	

Steps off the Pacific Coast Highway, five miles north of Santa Monica in a dilapidated wooden shack surrounded by a gravel lot and facing a panoramic sunset sea, this drafty dining room earned its success the old-fashioned way: by serving excellent, low-priced Thai food in generous portions, using the freshest ingredients. Cholada reels in a wild bunch of Malibu swells, beach bohemians and others willing to burn time and gas in the chronic traffic jams on Highway 1 to get here.

Once arrived, some get no further than appetizers like wraps of steamed rice skins filled with fresh raw vegetables and served with a sweet dip of crushed roasted peanuts and fish sauce. Garlic, curry and chilies power up traditional Thai entrées of chicken, fish and shrimp.

Drago

014

Italian

2628 Wilshire Blvd. (bet. Princeton & 26th Sts.)

Phone:	310-828-1585	Mon – Fri lunch & dinner
Web:	www.celestinodrago.com	Sat – Sun dinner only
Prices:	$$$	

Born in 1991, Drago spawned a mini-empire of restaurants for chef-entrepreneur Celestino Drago, who stakes his fortune on premium products, skillful preparation and polished service.

Food and family figure prominently in his epicurean philosophy, which is no surprise since the chef originally hails from Sicily. You can taste his heritage in dishes such as *panzanella*, a rustic salad of toasted bread cubes, mozzarella, heirloom tomatoes and olives; a pumpkin tortelloni bathed in a fragrant sage cream; and, for dessert, ricotta-filled cannoli dipped in chopped pistachio nuts and orange marmalade.

Expensively conservative, the dining room abounds with leather and suede in muted colors, attracting a sophisticated business crowd for lunch.

Giorgio Baldi

015

I t a l i a n

114 W. Channel Rd. (off Pacific Coast Hwy.)

Phone:	310-573-1660	Tue – Sun dinner only
Web:	www.giorgiobaldi.com	
Prices:	**$$$$**	

This gleaming white cottage at the seaside mouth of Santa Monica Canyon resembles a Hamptons' hideaway and caters to an equivalently affluent local crowd, including celebrities drawn from Malibu and the posh residential heights above.

Chef-owner Giorgio Baldi pulls out all the stops, serving a fluffy crêpe topped with fine slices of smoked salmon in a pool of melted butter. A whole roasted lobster (an evening special) is a case study in rustic perfection: the meat removed, cut into bite-size lumps and tossed with sweet, roasted Italian plum tomatoes and leaves of freshly torn oregano and basil, then drizzled with olive oil. Then back into the shell, onto a platter, and placed before you.

Parking is scarce, so let the valet deal with it.

The Hump

016

J a p a n e s e

3221 Donald Douglas Loop S. (off Airport Ave.)

Phone:	310-313-0977	Tue – Fri lunch & dinner
Web:	www.thehump.biz	Mon & Sat – Sun dinner only
Prices:	**$$$$**	

Perched three flights above the Santa Monica Airport runway, named for the slang term American pilots used for the Eastern Himalaya during World War II, the restaurant's vintage lantern light fixtures, Asian ceiling panels, and revolving fans evoke other days, when the world seemed bigger and its dangerous places more romantic.

The cockpit of this spiffy hideaway is its 12-seat sushi bar. (Window tables and an outdoor terrace, however, command a panorama of the runway. Only the best, freshest ingredients will do for the sushi and sashimi, some flown in from Japan. The chef's-choice *omakase* is a straight flight path to the best the house can offer at the moment. Cooked seafood dishes are equally lofty.

JiRaffe

Californian ✗✗

017

502 Santa Monica Blvd. (at 5th St.)

Phone:	310-917-6671	Dinner daily
Web:	www.jirafferestaurant.com	
Prices:	**$$$**	

Chef-owner Raphael Lunetta was a dedicated surfer before catching his life's big wave. That's as Californian as you can be, and so is his casually elegant bistro on the last few blocks of old Route 66. Big windows flood the airy main floor and loft with light, and the chef's affable presence fills it with bonhomie.

Menus change often, nightly specials showcasing seasonal produce, seafood and meats. That can mean a white-corn soup with Dungeness crab meat, or roasted salmon with Meyer lemon-infused couscous, served with carrots, squash, onions and cauliflower roasted in a tomato-based broth. Desserts reflect seasonal fruit harvests.

Monday nights present a prix-fixe bistro menu, a bit more French than Californian. Reservations are advised.

Josie

American ✗✗✗

019

2424 Pico Blvd. (at 25th St.)

Phone:	310-581-9888	Dinner daily
Web:	www.josierestaurant.com	
Prices:	**$$$$**	

The street fronting Josie honors Pío Pico (1801-94), last governor of Mexican California. In his Los Angeles tavern, he sold drinks in hollowed-out ox horns with false wooden bottoms. By the 1850s he was one of the province's wealthiest men, known for posh living and devil-may-care ventures that eventually returned him to the ranks of the poor. Josie's shades-of-gray dining room and its formally uniformed staff would have suited Don Pió in his heyday.

And so would the fancy menu, with appetizers of frogs' legs, seared baby cuttlefish and roasted merguez lamb sausage, and entrées of sturgeon, duck, venison, and a buffalo "burger" crowned with foie gras. Josie enjoys a reputation it may not always live up to, but its patrons remain loyal.

Joe's ✤

Californian 🍴🍴

1023 Abbot Kinney Blvd.
(bet. Main St. & Westminster Ave.), Venice

Phone: 310-399-5811   Tue – Sun lunch & dinner
Web: www.joesrestaurant.com
Prices: $$$

Mike Eller/Crew Creative

Santa Monica Bay

Interior design is not the strong suit of this Venice ingénue,
favored by a mostly upscale, mostly young set, who ignore
the crowded tables and the noisy acoustics in favor of
chef Joe Miller's innovative and ambitious compositions.
Rightly, it is all about the food, a pleasure enhanced by
the unpretentious atmosphere inside Joe's small, one-story
stucco building.

You'll find refinement here, as in an amuse-bouche (small
bites before the meal to "amuse the mouth") of parsnip
soup with warm pancetta, or sautéed shrimp dusted with
ground *togashi* pepper. So, too, a poached duck foie gras
and a foie gras mousse over a granola honey biscuit; or
a succulent roasted leg and breast of organic chicken,
presented on a bed of baby bok choy with purées of
chestnut and mild red chile.

The friendly staff is earnest and attentive, if not sticklers
for detail.

Appetizers	*Entrées*	*Desserts*
• Lobster and Avocado, Lemongrass-Persian Mint Gelée	• Red Snapper, Potato Scales, Crispy Spinach	• Bay Leaf Panna Cotta, Lemon Gelée, Strawberry Ice Cream
• Tuna Tartare, Smoked Salmon, Cucumber, Tomato and Lemon Oil	• Vegetable "Breaded" Monkfish, Coconut-Curry Gastrique	• Rhubarb Soup, Strawberry Bread Pudding, Ginger Ice Cream
• Porcini Ravioli, Mushroom Parmesan Broth	• Beef Sirloin, Crispy Artichokes, Brown Butter Balsamic Vinaigrette	

La Botte

Italian ✕✕

020

620 Santa Monica Blvd. (at 6th St.)

Phone: 310-576-3072
Web: www.labottesantamonica.com
Prices: $$$

Mon – Fri lunch & dinner
Sat – Sun dinner only

Stefano De Lorenzo/La Botte

It's difficult to imagine a warmer interior than in this homey yet fashionable place, which pays homage to Italian wine with its hardwood floors and walls crafted from the staves of oak wine barrels (a nod to the name, Italian for "wine barrel"). Authentic, one thinks correctly, starting with a skilled and menu-savvy Italian-speaking staff able to debone a branzino tableside, and a well-timed kitchen whose homemade pasta proves delectable.

Bold flavors and delicious sauces sparkle in such refined Northern Italian recipes as house-made wild-boar sausage; pappardelle with braised-duck ragù; and creamy white-corn soup stocked with buttery lobster meat. To gild the lily, the chef may even step out of the kitchen to sprinkle truffle dust over your plate of pasta.

The purview of co-owner Stefano De Lorenzo, the wine cellar reflects a list that is *molto* serious.

Appetizers	*Entrées*	*Desserts*
● Sea Urchin and Mediterranean Sea Bass Carpaccio	● Cortinese Red Beet-Stuffed Pasta, Brown Butter, Parmesan	● Chocolate Mousse with Crunchy Chocolate Hazelnut Crust
● Sliced Celery and Artichokes, Arugula, Parmesan, and Lemon Dressing	● Beet Tagliolini, Quail Sausage, Parmesan Fondue	● Amaretto Semifreddo
● Sweetbreads, Soft Polenta, Marsala Sauce	● Duck, Foie Gras and Cabbage Ravioli, Fresh Truffle	● Neapolitan Grano Pie

Lares

021

Mexican 🍴🍴

2909 Pico Blvd. (bet. 29th & 30th Sts.)

Phone: 310-829-4559 Lunch & dinner daily
Web: www.laresrestaurant.com
Prices: 💰💰

To step into the tiled downstairs dining room is to go back in time to the *cantinas* of old, reincarnated here with Mission-style furniture, an ornately carved bar, sunny plaster walls and a beamed ceiling. To be welcomed by *señoritas* in flowing skirts and off-the-shoulder blouses, perhaps also by a flamenco guitarist, completes the journey.

In Alta California, supper-table hospitality was a hacienda's measure, however humble. But here even the most familiar dishes are proud. A chicken enchilada, served in corn tortillas with tomato and chile-powder-scented rice and pinto beans flavored with white onions, oozes with melted cheese and is topped with a tangy *salsa verde* redolent of cilantro and Mexican oregano. You should feel welcome.

La Serenata De Garibaldi

022

Mexican 🍴🍴

1414 4th St. (at Santa Monica Blvd.)

Phone: 310-656-7017 Lunch & dinner daily
Web: www.laserenataonline.com
Prices: 💰💰

A great choice for a casual meal, La Serenata is well located near Third Street Promenade. Old Mexico comes to life in the hacienda-style interior, with its warm gold and orange tones, and elaborate wrought-iron accents. Real flower-filled window boxes festoon faux windows painted on one wall of the charming dining space.

Fresh ingredients light up dishes like comforting lima-bean soup, and *tacos blandos*, topped with shredded roasted chicken, crisp lettuce, creamy guacamole and piquant garlic-tomatillo sauce.

Although street parking is limited in this area, you will find several parking garages nearby. La Serenata, part of a small group of local eateries, has two other locations in LA *(1842 E. 1st St. and 10924 W. Pico Blvd.).*

Santa Monica Bay

Le Petit Café

2842 Colorado Ave. (at Stewart St.)

Phone:	310-829-6792	Mon – Fri lunch & dinner
Web:	N/A	Sat dinner only
Prices:	**$$**	

Appealing French provincial décor (nobody really notices) and simple French café food (everybody really notices) sum up the story of chef-owner Robert Bourget's cheery cottage-like restaurant, set off by itself in a commercial neighborhood. Painted Provençal plates decorate the walls; chalkboards list the choices; small tables draped with flower-patterned cloths fill the room. Farther back is an open kitchen, then a line of hallway tables leading to a rear dining area.

Dishes are *très Français*, with appetizers citing pâté, and *plats principaux* including duck confit and steak *au poivre*. A chicken breast well seasoned with pepper and fresh Provençal herbs is served in a creamy Dijon-mustard sauce. Fresh berry tarts proclaim that spring has arrived.

The Lobster

Seafood

024

1602 Ocean Ave. (at Colorado Ave.)

Phone:	310-458-9294	Lunch & dinner daily
Web:	www.thelobster.com	
Prices:	**$$$**	

The leap from a neighborhood seafood shack to a big Postmodern platform on the bluff overlooking the Santa Monica Pier wasn't easy, but the people who replaced the closed-down relic with the new Lobster have revived the original's reputation for great American seafood featuring whole live Maine lobsters and much of whatever else crawls or swims beneath the sea.

Lobster flavors clam chowder, the creamy sauce sparked with applewood-smoked bacon. Lobster also tops salads and fills sandwiches. As an entrée, the crustacean comes steamed or grilled by the pound. Landlubbers can resort to grilled chicken or steak.

As for the ocean view, it's stellar. Just below lies the pier's carousel building, a National Historic Landmark dating from 1916.

Santa Monica Bay

Locanda del Lago

Italian

231 Arizona Ave. (at 3rd St.)

Phone:	310-451-3525
Web:	www.lagosantamonica.com
Prices:	$$$

Lunch & dinner daily

If you're wondering which *lago*, it's Northern Italy's Lake Como. The menu showcases recipes from the lakeside city of Bellagio and environs. Take a seat in this bistro on the busy pedestrian-only Third Street Promenade, with its rustic wood tables and warm golden walls, and you could be in Lombardy.

Watch the chefs in the open kitchen prepare such Lago di Como traditions as *trota alla Comasca*, fillet of rainbow trout marinated in lemon juice, salty capers and fresh parsley, and served atop potato slices draped in melted cheese. This is hearty fare, like the *ribollita*, a Tuscan soup of chicken broth, smoky cannellini beans, *cavolo nero* and minced vegetables, topped with parmesan cheese and croutons. The wine list favors fine Italian vintages.

Michael's

American

1147 3rd St. (at Wilshire Blvd.)

Phone:	310-451-0843
Web:	www.michaelssantamonica.com
Prices:	$$$$

Mon – Fri lunch & dinner
Sat dinner only

Going on 30, this survivor has seen many contemporaries fail to launch. But founder Michael McCarty believed that a smart gallery look (including A-list art), a seasonal menu of "modern American cooking" with high-quality ingredients, a well-trained staff and smart promotion would boost his namesake into orbit. It did, and the restaurant, its interior little changed, enjoys a long-standing, well-heeled following of regulars who know to ask for a table on the tented garden patio.

Starters run the gamut: yellowtail sashimi; a fig and goat-cheese salad cradling a balsamic-vinegar-based fig confiture; an artisan foie gras. Main courses span the 50 states, from Maine diver scallops and lobster to a Sonoma County duck breast, or an Alaskan halibut.

Mélisse ✿✿

French 𝕏𝕏𝕏

1104 Wilshire Blvd. (at 11th St.)

Phone:	310-395-0881	Tue – Sat dinner only
Web:	www.melisse.com	
Prices:	**$$$$**	

Edward Duarte/Mélisse

Named for a lemon-scented Mediterranean herb, Mélisse is the studio of chef/owner Josiah Citrin, who opened the restaurant with his wife, Diane, in 1999. Deliciously highlighting the natural flavors of the market's best products, each of Citrin's *chef d'oeuvres* reflects a refined hand and a thoughtful composition. An amuse-bouche may take a sculptural form, as in a small cylindrical glass layered with tomato gazpacho and avocado gelée. Memorable pairings might include a seared Maine diver scallop on a plate painted with swirls of sweetly floral hibiscus reduction, or an earthy, roasted Liberty Farms duck breast set off by Californian Black Mission figs and a sweet-and-sour *jus* of both.

A burgundy carpet and creamy walls coupled with soft lighting soothe the mood. Valet parking is offered behind the restaurant, off 11th Street, where you'll enter into the bar area.

Appetizers	*Entrées*	*Desserts*
• Sweet Onion-Parmesan Soup, Crab Cake, Meyer Lemon	• Prime Beef "A la Moutarde", Potato Galette, Béarnaise	• Sticky Toffee Pudding, Mocha Malt Ice Cream, Coffee "Tia Maria", Orange Consommé
• Egg Caviar, Poached Egg, Lemon-Chive Crème Fraîche, American Osetra	• Olive-crusted Lamb Loin and Shank, Fennel, Peruvian Potatoes	• Frozen Passionfruit Parfait, Coconut Sorbet, Lemongrass

Moonshadows

028

20356 Pacific Coast Hwy. (west of Big Rock Dr.), Malibu

Phone:	310-456-3010
Web:	www.moonshadowsmalibu.com
Prices:	$$$

Lunch & dinner daily

The chatterbox crowd at this oceanfront Malibu veteran often suggests a reunion of recent college grads. Look again and you'll see a range of people, all of whom come for the delicious food, the exhilarating panorama and soothing rush of surf below the open-air deck. The place recalls a '70s hangout, with its cobalt-blue bar and dated architecture, but the kitchen is first-rate, using the finest local products to turn out inspired cuisine.

While fish from near and far are featured, the fare is solidly American—as in filet mignon, pork chops, short ribs, free-range chicken, and a Kobe beef burger layered in slices of caramelized onion and ripe tomato.

At night, the young elite show up to toast to the amazing sunsets.

Nobu

029

3835 Cross Creek Rd. (off Pacific Coast Hwy.), Malibu

Phone:	310-317-9140
Web:	www.nobumatsuhisa.com
Prices:	$$$$

Dinner daily

Set in a back corner of the Malibu Country Mart, a low-slung complex of shops, galleries and restaurants, this convivial local favorite offers sushi-bar seating and outdoor tables on a screened and tented patio. Nobu is, of course, another jewel in the crown of acclaimed sushi master Nobu Matsuhisa.

A chorus of chefs greets you as you enter, and a knowledgeable corps of waiters attends to every detail. The menu balances sushi and raw fish with cooked dishes; all are executed with precision and skill. Nobu-style ceviche calls for bite-size pieces of raw octopus, squid, shrimp and tuna mixed with crunchy shaved daikon, carrot and cucumber and spiced with a citrus vinaigrette, while Chilean sea bass may be glazed in a salty-sweet black-bean sauce.

Ocean Avenue Seafood

Santa Monica Bay

030

1401 Ocean Ave. (at Santa Monica Blvd.)

Phone: 310-394-5669 — Lunch & dinner daily
Web: www.oceanave.com
Prices: $$$

The name tells you what to expect: a prime Santa Monica location overlooking the Pacific, spectacular sunset views from the glass-enclosed stone terrace, a convivial raw bar starring oysters flown in from around the world.

Fish offerings run from a smoked trout fillet to a Japanese-inspired black cod flavored with sweet-salty sake *kasu*, the tasty refined remnant of the rice used to make the wine. At times, the crush of crowds can take a toll on service.

Said to derive from the 1920s English colonial style in Bali and Indonesia, the décor sets natural colors against white oak and cherrywood floors. You'll also spot Honduras mahogany panels and Hawaiian koa wood detailing, with mosquito net drapery here and a Madagascar straw ceiling there.

One Pico

Californian

031

1 Pico Blvd. (at Ocean Ave.)

Phone: 310-587-1717 — Lunch & dinner daily
Web: www.shuttersonthebeach.com
Prices: $$$$

Although it resides in a stately lodge-like room staring out at the ocean from Shutters on the Beach *(see hotel listing)*, One Pico doesn't rely on its stellar views to attract diners. The delicious seasonally changing California cuisine does that.

Dishes allow superior ingredients to state their case. As such, roasted Santa Barbara mussels come in a fragrant cream-enriched broth of their own cooking liquid; and grilled swordfish is seasoned simply with salt and pepper, and served with a tomato fondue.

A stone fireplace and wrought-iron chandeliers give the airy room a rustic feel, with tall windows opening out onto the beach. It's a room where business-casual attire feels right, and flip-flops and T-shirts—de rigueur on the sand—do not.

The Penthouse

032

Contemporary

1111 2nd St. (at Wilshire Blvd.)

Phone: 310-393-8080
Web: www.thehuntleyhotel.com
Prices: $$$

Lunch & dinner daily

If heaven had a members-only club, it might look like this restaurant in The Huntley Hotel *(see hotel listing)*, where white fabric and leather dominate and views sweep across the Santa Monica Bay. Come evening, the night-club ambience is palpable with its pulsing music, and throngs of A-listers and chic wannabes vying for seats at the circular bar.

Without the kitchen's culinary prowess you couldn't pull off a "Green Crunch" salad of fresh raw asparagus, snap peas, green beans and edamame. You might botch the fruity pomegranate vinaigrette, and probably wouldn't get a roasted Kurobuta pork shank with sweet roasted yams and cherry sauce just right.

You'll be more at ease, up here on the 18th floor, if you dress with a bit of style.

Piccolo

033

Italian

5 Dudley Ave. (off Speedway), Venice

Phone: 310-314-3222
Web: www.piccolovenice.com
Prices: $$$

Dinner daily

The healthy fare at this small neighborhood haunt (sister to La Botte in Santa Monica) sacrifices no flavor for its lightness. Chefs here are journeymen steeped in native skill. Fine slices of a duck prosciutto get a garnish of gorgonzola cream and olive oil, the meat's flavors drawn out by cracked pepper and sea salt. *Pesce* vary with the day, but preparation is consistently excellent, as in a baked black cod with a crust of reduced balsamic vinegar and dry mustard, covered with diced sweet tomatoes and torn arugula. Furnishings are simple, and Italian is spoken in the open kitchen, resonating off the red tile floors.

Take Rose Avenue to the beach and park in the public lot. Allow time, since seating is on a first-come, first-served basis.

Santa Monica Bay

Primitivo Wine Bistro

Mediterranean

034

1025 Abbot Kinney Blvd. (near Main St.), Venice

Phone: 310-396-5353
Web: www.primitivowinebistro.com
Prices: $$$

Mon – Fri lunch & dinner
Sat – Sun dinner only

Tapas make up the menu at this urban-bohemian Venice bistro. The location accounts for the thirty-something crowd who, come evenings, create a noisy mixer with the added fun of sampling wines from all points of the compass rose.

The house bets on pairing wine with tapas; given that the list of both is long and that the former includes a wide selection of flights, the odds favor the house. Since these dishes evolved into mini-entrées in the States, tapas have gotten fancy. You might see a steak carpaccio sprinkled with sliced shallot and capers, Medjool dates wrapped in bacon, sautéed Tiger shrimp in a garlic-scented broth, or a seared sea bass topped with a butternut-squash purée. For those who find menu choices difficult, this is a forgiving place.

Real Food Daily

035

Vegan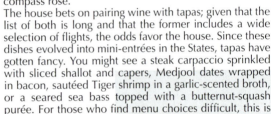

514 Santa Monica Blvd. (at 5th St.)

Phone: 310-451-7544
Web: www.realfood.com
Prices:

Lunch & dinner daily

It's good diet advice. Here (and at the West Hollywood location at 414 N. La Cienega Blvd.) it translates into vegan fare—no animal products at all. That also means baked goods without fats or sugars, when possible, and strictly organic ingredients. Despite these self-imposed rules, the food is flavorful and satisfying, packing in the health-conscious to fill the small dining room, the kitchen counter seats and the upstairs area.

Vegan sparks skepticism in some, but try the vegetable roll, an al dente rice-flour wrap stuffed with a cilantro-scented mélange of yellow squash, zucchini, carrot and radish; or a burrito of Spanish rice, black beans, smoky soy bacon, jalapeño tofu cheese and avocado—you'll find no sacrifice to the kitchen's code.

Rustic Canyon

036

Californian ✗✗

1119 Wilshire Blvd. (bet. 11th & 12th Sts.)

Phone: 310-393-7050
Web: www.rusticcanyonwinebar.com
Prices: $$$

Mon – Fri lunch & dinner
Sat – Sun dinner only

Dark beams, buttery walls, and a wood bar evoke the Southwest, here with a Moderne flair. The real Rustic Canyon is a wild, deep groove in the nearby Santa Monica Mountains, where the ruins of an early 20th-century artist colony remain. Communal tables encourage that kind of group interaction, while booths set in alcoves afford privacy.

Seasonal SoCal cuisine marries well with selections from the extensive wine list, which roams the continents for inspiration. A generous choice by the glass starts with bubbly and ends with ruby Port. Simple food combinations show off the kitchen's talent in the likes of thick slices of rare filet mignon served atop grilled artisan bread, the meat spiced with a thin layer of horseradish-infused cream.

Sam's by the Beach

037

International ✗✗

108 W. Channel Rd. (off Pacific Coast Hwy.)

Phone: 310-230-9100
Web: N/A
Prices: $$$

Tue – Sun dinner only

In an unassuming cottage, steps from where the Santa Monica Canyon meets the Pacific Coast Highway, this cozy, casual-chic citizen of the world serves Mediterranean food with influences from California, the Continent, and the Middle East.

The skillful melding works well. Calamari is coated here with a piquant spice-rub of cayenne pepper, paprika, cumin, garlic, sumac and turmeric, grilled to marvelous tenderness, and presented alongside spicy watercress dressed in olive oil and lemon juice. Desserts, like a phyllo "bird nest" filled with rosewater-scented milk pudding and sprinkled with roasted chopped pistachios, may adopt a Middle Eastern flair.

Valet parking is your only option on this heavily trafficked street.

Sapori

Italian

038

13723 Fiji Way (in Fisherman's Village), Marina del Rey

Phone: 310-821-1740   Lunch & dinner daily
Web: www.sapori-mdr.com
Prices: **$$**

Only a sidewalk separates this cheerful tenant of Marina del Rey's Fisherman's Village from the harbor's channel to the sea, where yachts glide by in stately procession. On warm days the sheltered outdoor patio, with its ocean-scented breezes and serene maritime vista, induces languorous states of mind.

Fine flavors (*sapori* in Italian) reign in the uncomplicated and tasty dishes. A variety of olives marinated in olive oil, vinegar and spices makes a good place to start before moving on to the likes of grilled jumbo prawns marinated in herbs and lemon juice, and served with rosemary-roasted potatoes and skewered grilled vegetables. If you're a coffee lover, round out your meal with a traditional *affogato*, vanilla gelato drowned in espresso.

Shima

Japanese

039

1432 Abbot Kinney Blvd. (at Milwood Ave.), Venice

Phone: 310-314-0882   Tue – Sat dinner only
Web: N/A
Prices: **$$**

A sheet of paper taped to a wooden gate is the only clue to Shima's presence in a two-level town house beyond. Inside, molded chairs and sushi-bar stools daub color on a subdued palette of gray concrete and white walls.

Veneration of the sushi craft underlies the devotion to presentation using the freshest ingredients. That's made clear by the taste of silky-smooth house-made tofu served in a pool of tangy soy sauce, topped with grated ginger and sliced scallions. Sashimi and brown-rice sushi are signature items here. Thus bluefin tuna is lightly seared, topped with shredded daikon, micro greens and finely shaved pieces of raw garlic. Brown rice, with its chewy texture and earthy, nutty flavor, elevates simple rolls to ineffable heights.

3 Square Café & Bakery

Bakery ✗

040

1121 Abbot Kinney Blvd. (at San Juan Ave.), Venice

Phone: 310-399-6504
Web: www.rockenwagner.com
Prices: $$

Tue – Sat lunch & dinner
Mon & Sun lunch only

Venice has plenty of casual dining spots, but this one is a step above the rest. Among the baked goods here are the wonderful signature pretzel rolls studded with coarse salt. It's this roll that accounts for the popularity of the pretzel burger, topped with melted Swiss and caramelized onions.

This airy cafe has floor-to-ceiling windows and tables whose planks extend through openings in a glass wall to the patio. The owner's German roots influence the menu, hence apple pancakes with crème fraîche, and *leberkäs* (Bavarian breakfast meatloaf) made with eggs, Bavarian mustard and, of course, a pretzel roll.

This isn't a place to count calories; the likes of a luscious vanilla-bean cheesecake are too good to pass up.

Tra di Noi

041

Italian ✗✗

3835 Cross Creek Rd. (off Pacific Coast Hwy.), Malibu

Phone: 310-456-0169
Web: N/A
Prices: $$

Lunch & dinner daily

Reliably good, with a mostly Malibu crowd who tend to be acquainted (*tra di noi* means "between us"), this colorful, comfortable and casual home-style *ristorante* in the Malibu Country Mart features classic dishes prepared simply with traditional flavors and fresh ingredients.

Lobster-and-crab cakes, for instance, come finely seasoned with a wonderfully matched sweet-tangy mango sauce swirled with a syrupy balsamic reduction. You could probably close your eyes, point to the menu, and be pleased with even humble dishes like the house gnocchi, smothered in an herb-infused tomato sauce and melted mozzarella, and garnished with shaved parmesan.

Umbrellas keep the sun off patio diners, who have a view of the adjoining park and playground.

Typhoon

Asian

042

3221 Donald Douglas Loop S. (off Airport Ave.)

Phone:	310-390-6565	Mon – Fri & Sun lunch & dinner
Web:	www.typhoon-restaurant.com	Sat dinner only
Prices:	$$	

Typhoon's second-floor view of Santa Monica Airport suits its menu, the origins of which lie far beyond the blue horizon. Chefs work with deft skill in an open kitchen, but eyes are drawn more to the small aircraft coming and going. The polished concrete floor, wood tables and chairs, and noisy acoustics banish pretense; this is a fun, convivial place.

Asian cuisines converge here, and the menu is locally notorious for its selection of insects—crickets, scorpions, waterbugs—delicacies in Asia. Large platters of whole fish accommodate families or groups. The only mistake possible with this fare is to over-order, for servings are generous. The popular bar appeals with its weather-chart background.

Via Veneto

Italian

044

3009 Main St. (bet. Marine St. & Pier Ave.)

Phone:	310-399-1843	Dinner daily
Web:	www.viaveneto.us	
Prices:	$$$	

If you can find a more romantic place, go there. Glimmering candles (the primary light source), a high ceiling, wooden wine racks, and gilt-framed mirrors on faux-finished, earth-tone walls take you halfway there. Charming Italians serving tasty dishes with traditional flavor combinations do the rest, or nearly so.

This is authentic cuisine: strips of earthy, roasted portobello mushrooms topped with shaved salty-sharp aged parmesan; a salt-crusted baked sea bass seasoned with sprigs of rosemary. As sweets for your sweet, a ricotta-cheese tart is dotted with plump, sweet raisins and finished with a dusting of powdered sugar.

After a wedding, bring your party back to the upstairs balcony room, which affords privacy to small groups.

Valentino ✿

Italian 🍴🍴🍴

3115 Pico Blvd. (bet. 31st & 32nd Sts.)

Phone:	310-829-4313	Mon – Thu & Sat dinner only
Web:	www.welovewine.com	Fri lunch & dinner
Prices:	$$$$	

Valentino Restaurant Group

Santa Monica Bay

The wine book, listing 2,500 labels, is as thick as the LA phone directory, which gives you a sense of the heft of Piero Selvaggio's much-praised flagship. (He has two more restaurants in Las Vegas). Conventional wisdom gushes over this place, while some grouse that the décor, billed as an "eclectic mix of stylish and timeless ambience," is merely dated. Valentino is what it is: lavish, pricey and nostalgic.

Selvaggio declares a dedication to freshness and the procurement of delicacies—cheese from Puglia, white truffles from the Piemonte, fish from the Mediterranean, organic farm-raised meats. His are traditional and rustic recipes; thus a perfectly executed oven-baked lasagnette incorporates a savory ragù of sausage and fresh tomatoes, perfumed with Maui onion purée and topped with pecorino cheese.

Desserts have a habit of stealing the show in the final act.

Appetizers	*Entrées*	*Desserts*
● Bolognese Lasagnetta, Quail Reduction Sauce	● Sautéed Cod, Red Pepper Sauce, Sichuan Pepper	● Bianco e Rosso: White Chocolate Mousse, Raspberry-Cherry Center
● Duckling and Tomato Crespelle, Mosto Cotto Reduction	● Lamb Osso Buco, Wilted Greens, Chanterelles	● Italian Rice Pudding, Strawberries, Balsamic Sorbet
● Sweet White Corn Tortelloni, Farmer's Market Vegetables	● Braised Veal Cheeks, Red Wine Sauce, Root Vegetables	● Amaretto-flavored Peaches in Phyllo

Violet

045

Californian

3221 Pico Blvd. (at 32nd St.)

Phone: 310-453-9113
Web: www.violetrestaurant.com
Prices: $$

Tue – Fri lunch & dinner
Sat & Sun dinner only

A violet neon light announcing the restaurant and banquettes that pop with violet upholstery tell you something's up here. Chef/owner Jared Simmons' small plates epitomize Californian cuisine; preparations here defer to the natural flavors of high-quality ingredients.

Silky corn soup tastes like ripe sweet corn, here sprinkled with diced green chives, and a dash of salt to accent the sweetness. A sandwich of house-cured salmon on toasted foccacia-like bread is punctuated with fresh dill and briny green capers. Changing entrées are to the point—say multicolored beets with smoked eel, steamed mussels, Ahi tuna tartare, or seared scallops.

There's a small European hotel-style bar, and a booth large enough to hold the writing staff of a sitcom.

Wabi-Sabi

046

Japanese

1637 Abbot Kinney Blvd. (at Venice Blvd.), Venice

Phone: 310-314-2229
Web: www.wabisabisushi.com
Prices: $$

Dinner daily

Industrial décor meets contemporary Japanese food at this boho-chic space on Venice's signature boulevard of shops and cafes. The gallery-style look (polished concrete floor, brick walls, track lighting, framed art) suits the neighborhood and the restaurant's name, a reference to the key physical and philosophical elements of traditional Japanese beauty, which seeks perfection while accepting its impossibility.

Sushi and sashimi, along with small plates and hot food, are crafted using traditional and modern approaches. That permits a sushi roll of baked warm crab meat to be paired with chunks of creamy avocado and a sweet rice-wine sauce, or shrimp potstickers to be served on a pool of carrot-ginger purée—a fine fusion of East and West.

Whist

047

Californian

1819 Ocean Ave. (at Pico Blvd.)

Phone:	310-260-7511	Lunch & dinner daily
Web:	www.viceroysantamonica.com	
Prices:	$$$	

Neo-English décor and a formal staff, not to mention a name that refers to an 18th-century card game, belie the fun of fine dining at the hip Viceroy Hotel *(see hotel listing)*. Seafood, steak and specialties made with familiar ingredients appear here in light and flavorful new combinations. A celebrity hotspot, the Viceroy is a stylish retreat with amenities galore, including Whist's cozy booths and outdoor poolside patio tables and cabanas, rendered romantic by candlelight.

There's show biz in a layered salad of poached persimmon topped with curly frisée; so, too, in a pan-roasted monkfish atop celery-root purée, roasted chanterelles and sweet kernels of yellow corn. There's star-gazing as well, both sideways and straight up.

Wilshire

048

Californian

2454 Wilshire Blvd. (at 25th St.)

Phone:	310-586-1707	Mon – Fri lunch & dinner
Web:	www.wilshirerestaurant.com	Sat dinner only
Prices:	$$$$	

This discreet, brown building is easy to miss, as is its adjoining valet-parking area. Inside, chocolate brown colors the leather of the bar's chairs and banquettes, as well as the wood floors and paneling; diaphanous fabric screens create a slightly fantastic feel. Heat lamps warm the multilevel open-air deck, which hosts a lively scene.

Warren Schwartz's à la carte menu changes with the availability of seasonal produce and other ingredients chosen for quality and cooked to accent their natural flavors and textures. There's no mistaking the components of diver scallops seared in clarified butter and served with creamy roasted fingerlings and spicy chorizo. The wine director's list is international, and fine labels are offered by the glass.

Santa Monica Bay

Ventura Boulevard

Agoura Hills, Calabasas, Westlake Village

Even though Los Angeles voters rejected a 2002 bid to let nearly two dozen unincorporated communities within the San Fernando Valley's 235 square miles form a separate city, most admit "The Valley" is distinct from LA. Indeed the Census Bureau finds the 1.75 million people living between the Sierra Madre, Santa Monica and San Gabriel mountains more affluent, more foreign-born, and more likely to find parking.

The Tongva were here for at least 2,000 years before the Spanish founded **Mission San Fernando** in 1797, and cattle ranchos with haciendas like the De La Osa Adobe at **Los Encinos State Historic Park** in Encino. By the 20th century, the valley's Mediterranean clime was producing a cornucopia of fruits, nuts and vegetables. Photoplays of Hollywood stars on rustic ranch-style spreads added cachet. Between 1945 and 1960, the exodus to the suburbs, along with booms in aerospace and other industries, quintupled the area's population.

SYCAMORES TO SITCOMS

Part of El Camino Real, the old mission road that Highway 101 follows west past Agoura Hills, Ventura Boulevard runs some 17 miles between Calabasas (named for its native wild pumpkins) through Woodland Hills—where in 1922 Victor Girard planted over 120,000 pepper, sycamore and eucalyptus trees—and the Cahuenga Pass near Universal City. Along the boulevard's busy lanes you'll now find the Valley's densest collection of small businesses, including popular Sushi Row in **Studio City** as well as restaurants serving a world of different cuisines.

Also in 1922, the area's first golf links opened at Ventura and Coldwater Canyon. Just east of

VENTURA BOULEVARD

150

Laurel Canyon Boulevard were Mack Sennett's Keystone Studios, a silent-movie laugh factory whose two-reelers featured Fatty Arbuckle, W. C. Fields, Stan Laurel and Oliver Hardy, and the Keystone Kops. The lot became Republic Pictures in 1935, where John Wayne and Roy Rogers created their cowboy personas. Today it hosts **CBS Studio Center** *(closed to the public)*, where TV sitcoms and dramas are produced.

Long used for filming street scenes, Ventura Boulevard (and the Sherman Oaks Galleria mall) gained iconic status in 1982 when Frank and Moon Unit Zappa's hit single "Valley Girl" ("On Ventura, there she goes...") introduced America to the dialect ("Like, *totally* awesome!"). Countering the boulevard's lowbrow stigma are avant-garde communities like North Hollywood's **NoHo Arts District** just north of **Universal Studios**. With more than 20 live theaters and dozens of galleries, dance studios, recording venues and clothing and specialty shops, Ventura is *totally* fun.

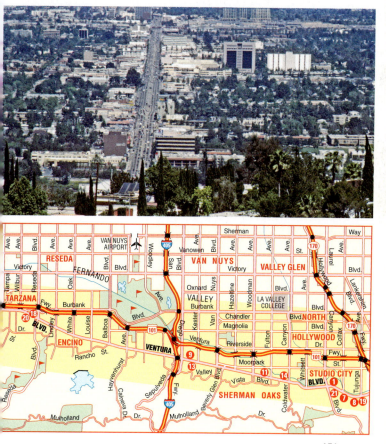

Asanebo ✿

001

11941 Ventura Blvd. (at Radford Ave.), Studio City

Phone: 818-760-3348
Web: N/A
Prices: $$$

Tue — Fri lunch & dinner
Sat — Sun dinner only

Ventura Boulevard

Asanebo

At this humble eatery, the friendly quartet of skilled sushi chefs enjoys a following of local regulars, who keep the small, minimally decorated strip-mall space hopping. Unlike some sushi and sashimi restaurants along Studio City's "Sushi Row," Asanebo offers a selection of delectable hot dishes. Daily specials featuring the freshest market fish are favored by habitués, many drawn from the nearby media and music-industry complexes.

The reasonably priced chef's *omakase* is the way to eat here; it shows off a wide range of flavors and textures based on excellent ingredients. Inspired combinations—a daub of sesame-miso paste and a slice of Serrano chile pepper on perfectly cut slices of yellowtail, a charred miso glaze on grilled black cod, a crunch of sea salt and a tang of citrus enhancing Japanese red snapper sashimi—elevate every dish. Service is splendid, the ambience serene.

Appetizers

- Baby Spinach with Sautéed Portobello Mushroom Salad
- Halibut, Shrimp, Shiitake and O-ba Leaf Fried Seafood Stick
- White Miso-marinated Chilean Sea Bass over a Butter Leaf

Entrées

- Seared Red Snapper, Savor of Japanese Cedar, "Kappo" Style Broth
- Kanpachi Sashimi, Sesame and Miso Sauce, Serrano, Yuzu
- Toro Tartare, Caviar, Sweet Red Miso

Desserts

- Homemade Black Sesame or Roasted Brown Tea Ice Cream

Banzai Sushi

002 **Japanese**

23508 Calabasas Rd. (at Valley Circle Blvd.), Calabasas

Phone:	818-222-5800	Mon – Fri lunch & dinner
Web:	www.banzaisushi.com	Sat – Sun dinner only
Prices:		

Located in the heart of Old Town Calabasas, this casual, popular spot offers a wide selection of innovative, boldly flavored specialty rolls. Chefs behind the L-shaped bar, where locals hover waiting for seats to open up, make sushi that's contemporary and fun, along with meals combining sushi, teriyaki and sashimi.

The Hawaiian roll, a Banzai specialty, is a California roll of shredded crab meat dressed in light mayonnaise, with creamy avocado and batons of cucumber, topped with sesame- and soy-accented deep-red tuna. Wrap large lumps of steamed lobster with those little green batons and steamed asparagus, garnish with crunchy beads of *tobiko* caviar, and you have the house lobster roll. There's a pleasant tree-shaded patio in front.

Brandywine

003 **European**

22575 Ventura Blvd. (at Fallbrook Ave.), Woodland Hills

Phone:	818-225-9114	Tue – Fri lunch & dinner
Web:	N/A	Mon & Sat dinner only
Prices:	$$$	

Nothing, including the small pink cottage sheltering this tiny low-ceilinged dining room, is conventional here. Not the pink-saturated décor suggesting a Victorian great-aunt's parlor, not the dried pink carnations, the rickety bookshelves holding old tomes, or the vintage tableware. Call it eccentric.

The bill of fare (chalked on a blackboard) is the thing. Dishes are made with quality ingredients and simply presented, yet with a dash of ambition—a Mediterranean white-bean and clam soup spiced with red chile flakes, cilantro, garlic and bacon; a breast of duck roosting on a mound of mashed potatoes; a Meyer lemon pudding soufflé curtsying in a purple plum compote. Expect only traditional continental European dishes at this old-fashioned place.

Café 14

004

Californian ✕✕

30315 Canwood St. (at Reyes Adobe Rd.), Agoura Hills

Phone: 818-991-9560   Tue – Sun dinner only
Web: N/A
Prices: $$$

A gourmet surprise, tucked into the back corner of Reyes Adobe Plaza, Café 14 is more refined than its name or location implies. A tented L-shaped patio wraps from the front to the side of the building, and the dining room is set about with muted taupe walls, framed mirrors, vintage posters and finely set tables.

Skillfully prepared, internationally influenced dishes use premium and savory seasonal ingredients. Those international accents flavor a salad crafted from crispy duck and ripe, sweet nectarines, accented with Thai basil and a drizzle of hoisin-infused vinaigrette. They also show up in salmon seared in the fat rendered from andouille sausage, then roasted and served with a sweet-potato sausage hash and Cajun butter sauce.

Giovanni Ristorante

005

Italian ✕✕

21926 Ventura Blvd. (at Topanga Canyon Rd.), Woodland Hills

Phone: 818-884-0243   Tue & Thu – Sun dinner only
Web: www.giovanniristorante.com   Wed lunch & dinner
Prices: $$

Cherished memories of a patriarch's 1929 odyssey from Southern Italy to America inspire the menu in this quaint, cottage-like family-friendly spot. Dishes are straightforward and generous, spotlighting tasty pasta. The dining room's pale gold walls, decorated with hand-painted plates and white linen-draped tables, create a homey ambience. A covered back patio adds a sense of ease in this busy neighborhood that's lean on good dining choices.

Pastas are presented with the option to mix any of them with a variety of vegetables and traditional sauces, from creamy to a spicy red sauce flavored with beef and pork. Hearty favorites include baked gnocchi in an herb-rich tomato sauce oozing with melted mozzarella. A luscious tiramisú takes the cake.

Hampton's

006

Californian

2 Dole Dr. (at Via Rocas), Westlake Village

Phone:	818-575-3000	Mon – Sat dinner only
Web:	www.fourseasons.com/westlakevillage	Sun lunch only
Prices:	$$$	

European-style abounds at Hampton's in the Four Seasons Westlake Village *(see hotel listing)*. You see it in the entry lined with cabinets filled with wine bottles, and in the semi-circular paneled dining room where windows look out on water splashing over boulders in the hotel gardens. Gold sofas and red tapestry armchairs ease up to spacious linen-topped tables, their deep colors matched by drapes and carpeting. Service is professional and attentive.

Culinary mastery is obvious in morel mushrooms sautéed in butter and rendered pork fat, served with crispy cubes of pork belly roasted until the fat is gone, as well as in a meaty snapper roasted in olive oil with baby artichokes, and garnished with a pale green olive-oil foam. A meal here is memorable.

Katsu-ya

007

Japanese

11680 Ventura Blvd. (at Colfax Ave.), Studio City

Phone:	818-985-6976	Mon – Thu lunch & dinner
Web:	www.sushikatsu-ya.com	Fri – Sun dinner only
Prices:	$$	

This is the firstborn of a small chain of siblings—the newest branches occupy Philippe Starck-designed spaces "over the Hill" in LA. People flock to all locations, though the small room in this Ventura strip mall is architecturally blah.

Those seated on the coveted sushi-bar stools and the hungry diners hovering behind them couldn't care less. Everyone's reading the handwritten menu of daily specials or watching the chefs prepare artistic dishes ranging from the traditional (halibut sushi) to innovations like crispy-rice sushi.

Fresh is standard, technique simple, flavorings bold—a halibut drizzled with a citrus ponzu sauce, a seared tuna steak wreathed in tangy Asian salsa—all served in a relaxed, family-friendly setting.

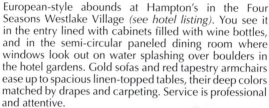

Ventura Boulevard

Kazu Sushi

Japanese ✕

008

11440 Ventura Blvd. (at Ridgemoor Dr.), Studio City

Phone:	818-763-4836	Mon – Fri lunch & dinner
Web:	N/A	Sat dinner only
Prices:	**$$$**	

With an unassuming strip-mall storefront, chef Kazu's place is small and modest, and he is sometimes alone behind his black-granite sushi bar, but his traditional sushi and sashimi offerings are fresh, simple and very good, an argument for taking the more expensive *omakase* option. The notion of "simple" sushi may seem redundant, but natural taste is the goal: a thin slice of *toro* (fatty tuna belly prized in Japan) is served on tender mounds of rice without garnish or sauce, letting its silky texture and buttery flavor speak for itself. A smear of wasabi on sushi rice offsets the sweetness of a cooked butterflied prawn. A small yuzu citrus garnish tops halibut sushi. For a stronger taste experience, ask the maestro for a spicy tuna hand roll.

La Pergola Ristorante

Italian ✕✕

009

15005 Ventura Blvd. (at Lemona Ave.), Sherman Oaks

Phone:	818-905-8402	Mon – Fri lunch & dinner
Web:	www.lapergolaristorante.net	Sat – Sun dinner only
Prices:	**$$$**	

Rustic and simple, with a charming Italian countryside décor of beamed ceilings and a tile floor, and a cadre of Italian-American regulars, La Pergola grows a large portion of the vegetables, fruits and herbs in the owner's adjoining *giardino organico*—the roasted figs and sun-dried tomatoes on your baguette likely traveled a mere 30 paces to your table. This garden adds farm-fresh spontaneity to the ever-changing fish, pasta, meat and poultry specials chalked up daily, which tend to trump the extensive printed menu. Either way, let the kitchen show off its skill at cooking fish, and save room for dessert.

If you've been admiring the lovely Italian pottery that decorates La Pergola, you can purchase pieces at the restaurant's ceramic shop.

156

Mandevilla

010

I n t e r n a t i o n a l ✗ ✗

951 S. Westlake Blvd.
(bet. Hampshire & Townsgate Rds.), Westlake Village

Phone:	805-497-8482	Mon – Fri lunch & dinner
Web:	www.mandevillarestaurant.com	Sat – Sun dinner only
Prices:	**$$$**	

At Mandevilla, hearty and flavorful dishes—the pastas in particular—have a strong Italian character, but also show American and international influences. The dining rooms' tawny walls and soft lighting, and touches like the brick-faced kitchen and exposed wine racks distance you from the modern shopping area outside. A tented and screened patio, with its green garden décor, takes you a bit farther.
A daily fish special supplements other seafood, poultry and meat entrées. Classics like an appetizer of oversized prawns perched on the rim of a cocktail glass, served with a horseradish cream and a tangy, tomato-based sauce—not to mention a New York-style cheesecake—add a touch of steakhouse flair to the old-school trattoria ambience.

Max

011

F u s i o n ✗ ✗

13355 Ventura Blvd. (bet. Dixie Canyon & Fulton Aves.), Sherman Oaks

Phone:	818-784-2915	Dinner daily
Web:	www.maxrestaurant.com	
Prices:	**$$$**	

Steps from traffic, beyond the tented sidewalk patio, the contemporary dining room's muted earth tones, plush carpet, leather banquettes, soft lighting and candles foster a tranquil sense of escape, even though a full house of tranquil escapees can be noisy.
Devotion to culinary craft makes for Cal-Asian dishes perfectly elaborated, with thoughtfully matched elements and delicate spicing. This is especially evident in appetizers like *lumpia*—shrimp and pork spring rolls with sweet-spicy chile dipping sauce and Asian slaw sparked with ginger and garlic—and in fish entrées such as broiled miso-marinated black cod served atop Asian vegetables and surrounded by a brown mushroom broth.
Valet parking is a must at this special-occasion restaurant.

Onyx

012

2 Dole Dr. (at Via Rocas), Westlake Village

Phone: 818-575-3000
Web: www.fourseasons.com
Prices: $$$

Dinner daily

A 2,000-gallon saltwater aquarium behind the front bar, translucent wall panels of semi-precious stone, bamboo floors and other striking Asian details render Onyx's space in the Four Seasons Westlake *(see hotel listing)* dramatic. A small sushi bar and a terrace dining area overlooking the hotel gardens and waterfall just gild the lily.

Diners well beyond hotel guests are attracted to chef Masa Shimakawa's specialties. His inspirations include a Hawaiian "poke" martini of diced tuna drizzled with red-chile oil, creamy avocado cubes and micro greens with truffle oil, garnished with wasabi-spiked flying-fish roe. A triumph of nuance, green-tea sea salt and a soy-based dipping sauce season sweet-potato tempura. Mild top-quality *toro* sushi is indeed a gem.

Panzanella

013

14928 Ventura Blvd. (at Kester Ave.), Sherman Oaks

Phone: 818-784-4400
Web: www.giacominodrago.com
Prices: $$$

Mon – Fri lunch & dinner
Sat – Sun dinner only

Typical fare at this member of Giacomino Drago's restaurant family runs to *scaloppini a piacere*, with a rich and tasty Marsala demi-glace, served with mashed potatoes and a bevy of delicately cooked small vegetables. Some get no further than the antipasti, making a meal of prosciutto and dried figs, beef carpaccio, marinated swordfish, goat-cheese-filled eggplant rolls, or a truffle-accented mushroom soufflé.

Italian wines are well represented. Desserts, as in a golden brown-butter tart filled with blackberries and served with vanilla ice cream, are Old Country rich.

By day, Panzanella hosts a business-lunch crowd. Come evening, a casual-chic clientele of couples and young families arrives. As always on Ventura, you must, as they say, valet.

Pinot Bistro

French ✕✕

014

12969 Ventura Blvd. (at Coldwater Canyon Ave.), Studio City

Phone: 818-990-0500
Web: www.patinagroup.com
Prices: $$$

Mon – Fri lunch & dinner
Sat – Sun dinner only

Imagine a provincial French farmhouse—on commercial Ventura Boulevard. Inside at least, the Patina Group pulls it off with rooms and alcoves paneled in dark wood, where cabinets display decorative ceramics, black banquettes line some walls, and a fireplace adds to the ambience.

At midday the vaulted room fills with a mix of retirees and young film executives from nearby Studio City, who come here to discuss their latest project over the likes of a slow-roasted pork sandwich with braised red cabbage, steak *frites*, or a lovely roasted trout sprinkled with diced bacon and smoky almonds. At dinner, the menu trades sandwiches for heartier fare.

Locals go Sunday nights for the weekly changing Sunday supper, a steal at three courses for under $30.

Riviera

Italian ✕✕✕

015

23683 Calabasas Rd.
(bet. Calabasas Pkwy. & Mulholland Dr.), Calabasas

Phone: 818-224-2163
Web: www.tuscany-restaurant.com
Prices: $$$

Mon – Fri lunch & dinner
Sat – Sun dinner only

When sunlight floods the front curtains, the gold walls, high-backed blue-and-beige-striped upholstered chairs, fine pale linens, shaded table lamps and deep-blue carpeting produce a peculiarly European mood in this contemporary dining room. You can't help but dream of foreign lands.

Consistency and flavor are winning cards here, and the house plays a skillful hand of classic Italian dishes using the finest ingredients. Tradition trumps tinkering. Thus an earthy medley of minced mushrooms stuffs a fillet of orange roughy. A salad special of *insalata caprese* (butter lettuce, beefsteak tomato and fresh mozzarella) may withhold the basil, but the herb's role is fulfilled by a tangy balsamic vinaigrette spiked with creamy chive dressing.

Saddle Peak Lodge ❀

A m e r i c a n

419 Cold Canyon Rd. (at Piuma Rd.), Calabasas

Ventura Boulevard

Phone:	818-222-3888
Web:	www.saddlepeaklodge.com
Prices:	**$$$$**

Wed – Fri dinner only
Sat – Sun lunch & dinner

Saddle Peak Lodge

A century-old retreat hard by its craggy namesake, this rustic log and stone lodge in brushy Las Virgenes Canyon is six miles from Malibu, and minutes from the suburbs of San Fernando Valley. Set among wooded slopes, the longtime Hollywood "in place" feels detached from modern times, save for the valet parkers who swarm around you on arrival.

Inside, a mix of guests from celebrities to couples celebrating special occasions animates the room. Hunting trophies line the walls, appropriate to a restaurant specializing in game, including elk (with chestnut *velouté*, bacon *lardons,* pearl onions and chive Spätzle), buffalo, venison, and squab (stuffed with sauerkraut, sweetbreads and foie gras). The word "feast" applies, especially to chef Steven Rojas' four-course tasting menu, paired with wines from the well-described list.

An organized brigade of servers manages to be attentive without being invasive.

Appetizers	*Entrées*	*Desserts*
● Pot de Crème Foie Gras with Brandied Cherry Marmalade and Fruit Nut Bread	● Filet Mignon with Pommes Purée "in" Bone Marrow, Yukon Potato and Smoked Bacon Terrine	● "Marshmallow S'more" with Cinnamon Graham Cracker and Grand Marnier Ganache
● Farmer's Market Egg Ravioli with Laura Chenel Goat Cheese and Mascarpone	● New Zealand Elk with Chestnut Velouté, Lardons, Pearl Onions and Chive Spätzle	● Chocolate Molten Cake with Espresso Ice Cream over Caramel and Chocolate Truffles

Suki 7

Japanese

925 Westlake Blvd. (bet. Hampshire & Townsgate Rds.), Westlake Village

Phone:	805-777-7579	Mon – Fri lunch & dinner
Web:	www.suki7lounge.com	Sat dinner only
Prices:	**$$$**	

Dramatic, contemporary Japanese ambience sets the stage for pretty dishes of sushi, sashimi and robata-grilled items here. Modish green armchairs provide nontraditional seating at the U-shaped sushi bar, while pulsing music and attractive servers play to a hip audience. It's anybody's guess whether the cool crowd comes for the bold décor or the delicious food.

The draw for most is the tasty food. Impeccable hand rolls make assertive use of flavor accents like spicy radish sprouts or red chile laced with sesame oil and chives. A signature miso-paste-glazed black cod is served on a swirl of creamy miso sauce and scallion-infused oil atop Swiss chard. Consider musty-sweet *shochu*, a barley-based traditional spirit, as an alternative to sake.

Sushi Iki

018

Japanese

18663 Ventura Blvd., Suite 106 (at Yolanda Ave.), Tarzana

Phone:	818-343-3470	Tue – Fri lunch & dinner
Web:	N/A	Sat – Sun dinner only
Prices:	**$$**	

This place serves oversized pieces of sushi from a short menu that's long on quality. Upping the ante on the run-of-the-mill sushi bar, the dining room boasts comfortable cushioned chairs, and cloth napkins and table runners. Sushi chefs chat and joke with customers as if they were old friends.

Fresh as can be is the overall impression. Neatly pressed rectangles of sushi rice with a thin layer of wasabi cushion large slices of albacore tuna and hamachi *toro* tarted up with grated yuzu zest. The tuna roll is spiced by mixing the minced fish with a dab of red-chile paste, sesame oil and scallions, the whole shebang rolled up with cucumber batons in toasted nori.

Parking options include a front lot and a garage in back of the shopping plaza.

Ventura Boulevard

Sushi Nozawa

Japanese

Ventura Boulevard

11288 Ventura Blvd. (at Eureka Dr.), Studio City

Phone: 818-508-7017   Mon – Fri lunch & dinner
Web: N/A
Prices: **$$$**

The supreme experience at this hole-in-the-wall is to sit at chef Kazunori Nozawa's small sushi bar, where a sign ("Trust Me") aptly states the arrangement known as *omakase* ("entrust" in Japanese). No menu is presented; the chef serves you what he chooses from his best ingredients. Nozawa's creations are simple and of the highest quality, making omakase the most popular option here.
Sashimi staple Ahi tuna comes flavored with a light *ponzu shoyu* (citrus) sauce and garnished with finely sliced scallions. Crisp seaweed wraps white crabmeat kept moist by a salty mayonnaise. Sushi is Tokyo-style (slightly warm rice, large slice of fish); halibut may have a layer of pungent wasabi, albacore a sprinkle of sliced scallions—or nothing at all.

Sushi Yotsuya

020

Japanese

18760 Ventura Blvd. (at Burbank Blvd./Crebs Ave.), Tarzana

Phone: 818-708-9675   Mon – Fri lunch & dinner
Web: N/A   Sat dinner only
Prices: **$$$**

Traditional excellence defines Masa Matsumoto's small sushi bar, where the affable chef will describe his creations for you. Traditional means just that: no spicy tuna or California roll, no popularized concoctions. Excellence includes devotion to craft and the freshest ingredients possible, the best argument for choosing Matsumoto's *omakase* menu, which changes daily.
What to expect? *Toro* (choice cuts of tuna belly), perhaps with onion shoots; a bite-sized piece of *hamachi* (yellowtail) with wasabi; *kanpachi* (a kind of yellowtail) paired with a fresh mint leaf; raw salmon covered with sweet miso-marinated kelp and toasted sesame seeds; and sticky rice scented with seasoned Japanese vinegar. Trust the master.

Tama Sushi

Japanese

11920 Ventura Blvd. (at Carpenter Ave.), Studio City

Phone: 818-760-4585
Web: www.tamasushi.net
Prices: $$

Mon – Sat lunch & dinner
Sun dinner only

Owner Katsu Michite is one of Los Angeles' most highly regarded sushi chefs, offering top-quality fare at notably modest prices. If you're of a mind for sushi or sashimi, there is little point in second-guessing Michite's daily *omakase* choices, which depend upon what he brings back from his pre-dawn trip to the market. With rice, a single platter of his picks can easily satisfy two appetites. The traditional lunch and dinner menus are extensive and tasty, but the venerable Japanese devotion to raw fish forms the soul of Michite's establishment—a rare Ventura Boulevard restaurant with private parking.

Tama Sushi's décor and furnishings are minimalist modern, with gentle colors and comfortable seating. Nothing distracts from the plate.

Ventura Boulevard

Westside

Brentwood, Century City, Culver City, West LA, Westwood

To many Angelenos "West LA" means everything within the city limits west of La Cienega Boulevard to the Pacific, from the Santa Monica Mountains south to Los Angeles International Airport. Most use the blanket term "Westside" to include everything regardless of municipal borders. All agree, however, that aside from its traffic jams, life on the sundown side of the Big Pueblo is something to be desired.

WESTSIDE REDUX

Brentwood and Pacific Palisades were once part of the 33,000-acre Mexican land grant known as Rancho San Vicente y Santa Monica. Parceled off after Mexico ceded California to the U.S. in 1848, the area's rolling woodlands and ocean breezes attracted developers taking cues from Beverly Hills by bordering streets with date palms and letting them follow the contours of the land. The aesthetic they instilled responded when the Depression shut down the Pacific Electric Railway's San Vicente Boulevard route (popular for seafood-dinner excursions to Playa del Rey), by replacing the tracks with its present grassy median of groomed coral trees running four miles from central Brentwood's restaurant row to the sea. The only downside to the Westside's sylvan nature—most accessible at **Will Rogers State Historic Park**, the humorist's former polo estate above Sunset in Pacific Palisades—became apparent in 1961 when the Great Bel-Air–Brentwood Fire,

the worst in Los Angeles history, destroyed 484 homes.

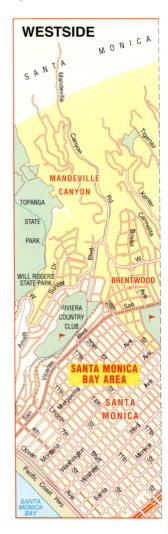

A Blend of Cultures

Though the residential enclaves within Century City, Holmby Hills, Westwood and Brentwood are less diverse, overall the Westside is cosmopolitan. It includes affluent African-American neighborhoods near Culver City, a Japanese-American community along Sawtelle Boulevard, and Latino neighborhoods in Palms. Brentwood and Westwood share a large Persian population. Each has restaurants that highlight cooking from the neighborhood's origin on the compass rose.

The Westside also boasts **The Getty Center**, whose hillside terraces afford a matchless panorama of nearly the entire 525-square-mile LA Basin.

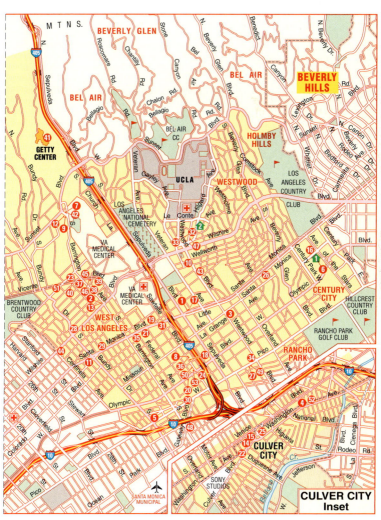

Angolo DiVino

001

11047 Santa Monica Blvd. (at S. Bentley Ave.)

Phone:	310-477-7080	Mon – Fri lunch & dinner
Web:	N/A	Sat dinner only
Prices:	**$$$**	

Tucked into a strip mall, the only choice open to many West LA eateries, Angolo DiVino hides its charm in its cozy neighborhood friendliness. The place is business-lunch boisterous by day, turning more romantic at night when lights are low. Being away from the Westside's touristy districts gives the place a certain calm, even though the presence of entertainment folk guarantees a buzz.

Simple combinations of fresh ingredients produce traditional dishes with Californian touches, as in a frisée salad coated with a tangy mayonnaise-based dressing and sprinkled with smoky cannellini beans, served alongside peppery grilled prawns. Thin-crust pizza is a lunchtime attraction, featuring the house tomato sauce. The wine list includes fine Italian labels.

Asakuma

002

11701 Wilshire Blvd. (at Barrington Ave.)

Phone:	310-826-0013	Lunch & dinner daily
Web:	www.asakuma.com	
Prices:	**$$**	

With locations on Santa Monica Boulevard, in Beverly Hills and in Marina del Rey geared toward take-out, this eat-in sibling is known for large portions of flavorful fare at very reasonable prices. That draws a big lunch crowd from surrounding highrises. At night, mostly locals fill the sushi bar and the simply decorated dining room.

The kitchen is deft, boosting the flavor of a miso soup with strips of caramelized tofu skin, scallions, seaweed and cubes of silken tofu. Salmon marinated in a spicy mix of chile paste, soy sauce and sesame oil is coated with crunchy *tobiko* and served as a salad. A marinade of sweet mirin and soy sauce, caramelized on black cod, is simply delicious.

Valet parking is the only option in the mall's tiny lot.

Baran

003

Persian

1916 Westwood Blvd. (at Missouri Ave.)

Phone: 310-475-4500   Lunch & dinner daily
Web: www.baranrestaurant.com
Prices:

Fine Persian dining in one of the world's largest expatriate communities is not as common as you'd expect. That's a key reason why this polite newcomer was quickly noted for its classic dishes mixing foreign flavors in interesting ways.

Baran's food is pleasantly mild, not overly spiced. The notion of a salad of diced raw cucumber, white onion and tomato, accented with chopped fresh mint and parsley, surprises with its refreshing crunchiness. What looks familiar, like a grilled chicken kabob, tastes exotic, flavored with onion, parsley and saffron. The marvelous sweet-tart taste of cherry rice (tender basmati cooked with tangy pitted cherries, rendering it pale violet in color) probably can't be done justice even in Farsi.

Beacon

004

Asian

3280 Helms Ave. (at Washington Blvd.), Culver City

Phone: 310-838-7500   Tue – Sat lunch & dinner
Web: www.beacon-la.com   Sun dinner only
Prices: $$ Mon lunch only

Like most spaces in the historic Helms Bakery complex, the former Beacon Laundry has a pleasing post-industrial look, with wood floors, high ceilings and tall windows. A bench runs the length of the table-crowded room, in addition to a small bar.

Thai and Chinese influences combine with European, yet the majority of dishes are Japanese. The Bento Box lunch, in a pretty lacquered box, offers a changing sampler of tastes and textures. You might find miso soup; seared albacore with ponzu sauce; grilled strips of chicken breast flavored with Thai green chile, lime leaves and fresh coriander; and a piece of smoky-sweet, miso-marinated black cod.

Consider combining your visit with a set at the nearby Jazz Bakery, one of LA's top music venues.

Bombay Café

005

12021 W. Pico Blvd. (at Bundy Dr.)

Phone:	310-473-3388	Mon – Fri lunch & dinner
Web:	www.bombaycafe-la.com	Sat & Sun dinner only
Prices:	$$	

With handmade naan, a hearty selection of appetizers, Indian beverages and daily specials, the menu here hovers above typical Indian fare. The list of starters includes exotica like a salad of diced cucumber, tomato and red onion, and *sev puri*, handmade crackers topped with smoky tomato chutney and beads of fried chickpea-flour batter. Pungently spiced lamb, stewed with sautéed onion slices, is cooled with a cucumber and yogurt *raita*. Memorably lush desserts encompass almond-flour *badaam* cake soaked in citrus-scented milk and served in a pool of spiced caramel.

In the skylit yellow room, rattan chairs, royal-blue wainscoting and a mirrored wood-and-brass bar evoke the Raj. Foliage shades the front windows, buffering the rush of traffic.

Breeze

006

2025 Ave. of the Stars (at Constellation Blvd.)

Phone:	310-551-3334	Lunch & dinner daily
Web:	www.centuryplaza.hyatt.com	
Prices:	$$$$	

On the lobby level of the Hyatt Regency Century Plaza *(see hotel listing)*, this kitchen's focus on fine ingredients and straightforward dishes sets it apart from most luxury-hotel restaurants. Rising amid Century City's office towers, Breeze does a brisk trade in business people, putting them at ease with friendly service.

Changing seasons and the region's agricultural and cultural variety determine the menu. Thus, at lunch, grilled Alaskan salmon might be paired with a rosemary-scented white-bean ragout. A crab cake starter at dinner is served with a dollop of garlic- and red-chile-infused aïoli, and garnished with plantain chips, while a thick slab of compound butter dominated by sharp Point Reyes blue cheese tops a seared filet mignon.

Brentwood
Restaurant & Lounge

American

148 S. Barrington Ave. (at Sunset Blvd.)

Phone:	310-476-3511	Dinner daily
Web:	www.brentwoodrestaurant.com	
Prices:	**$$$**	

Typically busy, with a bar catering to a young upscale crowd and a dining-room clientele spanning many generations, Brentwood's unassuming exterior belies its popularity and its good food.

American fare here goes multicultural, allowing tender yellow corn tortillas to be served open-face with slices of roasted Maple Leaf duck breast and drizzled with a pomegranate reduction, minced white onion and sprigs of cilantro. Almost as American as apple pie are the warm doughnuts with vanilla pastry cream and dark-chocolate dipping sauce.

The folks who frequent this hangout often congregate around the lively bar area. Know that the noise level can make conversation difficult, and a pen light could make you popular in the dimly lit dining room.

Chabuya

Japanese

2002 Sawtelle Blvd. (at La Grange Ave.)

Phone:	310-473-9834	Lunch & dinner daily
Web:	N/A	
Prices:		

A self-described Tokyo noodle bar, this simple café is one of the few places on the Westside where a good, filling meal of quality ingredients can be easily had for less than $20. Call this casual Japanese street food, as in a steamed, slightly sticky white bun smeared with a spicy-salty miso and red-chile sauce and wrapped around slices of fatty, smoky and tender roasted pork.

The house specialty is ramen, and the menu offers a wide selection of ramen-noodle combinations. Among the classics, a big bowl of steaming pork broth and noodles with sliced green scallions, crispy deep-fried onions, bamboo shoots, bean sprouts, and slices of roasted chicken *chashu*. Portions are so large that you could make a meal—with leftovers—on one bowl alone.

The Clay Pit

145 S. Barrington Ave. (at Sunset Blvd.)

Phone:	310-476-4700	Mon – Fri & Sun lunch & dinner
Web:	N/A	Sat dinner only
Prices:		

Westside

No-frills cooking using quality ingredients, simple décor cheered by yellow linens and walls faux-painted in gold and orange, modest prices and friendly service set the Clay Pit apart from other home-style restaurants in Los Angeles.

You may find some dishes a tad milder than classic Indian fare, but that can be remedied by request, adding bite to the likes of rice and peas *pullao*, delicately flavored with saffron and cardamom. Probably no boost will be required for a mashed and roasted eggplant stew flavored with white onions, garlic and ginger, and served with *channa* (garbanzo beans cooked in a spicy brown sauce sparked by chilies, garlic and ginger).

Buffet and prix-fixe options provide great value as well as a good sampling of dishes.

Danube

 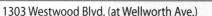
1303 Westwood Blvd. (at Wellworth Ave.)

Phone:	310-473-2414	Lunch & dinner daily
Web:	N/A	
Prices:		

In a storefront space off Wilshire Boulevard, Danube's décor is high émigré, with prints of traffic on the Danube, elbow-to-elbow tables draped in humble fabric, and cushioned wood chairs. There's a familial air here, with the staff chatting in Bulgarian and homeland music videos blaring from an overhead flat screen (a nod to expatriate regulars).

They must feel at home to find perfectly made *dolmas* flavored with olive oil and lemon, chopped sautéed onion and fresh herbs. To be able to dine on spicy *kufta* (falafel-sized patties of seared ground beef spiced with garlic, white onion and red-chile flakes) served with white rice saturated with salted butter, and finish with chocolate-layered *garash* cake, must make even the most stoic expat sigh.

Darya

Persian ✗✗

011

12130 Santa Monica Blvd. (at Bundy Dr.)

Phone:	310-442-9000	Lunch & dinner daily
Web:	www.daryarestaurant.com	
Prices:	**$$**	

Though it may seem gaudy to some, Darya's grand dining room, with its columns, crystal chandeliers and gilded mirrors, is opulent in a style more associated with days gone by in a cherished Persian homeland.

Richly flavored and authentic, nostalgic dishes please patrons from West Los Angeles' large Persian community. Charbroiled on a skewer, a marinated chicken breast takes on a bright yellow hue from turmeric and saffron. Imagine it served with *albolo polo*, basmati rice cooked with stewed black cherries and cherry juice. Baklava, saturated in sweet floral rosewater syrup, is irresistibly delicious.

Located off busy Santa Monica Boulevard, in a commercial strip, Darya is more easily accessed from the parking lot behind the restaurant.

Divino

Italian ✗✗

012

11714 Barrington Ct. (bet. Barrington & Sunset Aves.)

Phone:	310-472-0886	Lunch & dinner daily
Web:	N/A	
Prices:	**$$$**	

Nestled in Brentwood Village, Divino divides its space between a spacious, airy dining room and a little outdoor terrace. Though the latter overlooks the parking lot, flower boxes and pots of flowering plants perk up the ambience.

Redolent with fresh high-quality ingredients, savory pastas, thin-crust pizzas, and chicken dishes—especially the *pollo Portofino* (a boneless breast of chicken served with a sauce made with tomatoes, capers and olives)—headline here. Don't ignore the daily specials, which complement the classics with the likes of seared salmon picatta served in a butter sauce made tangy by the addition of lemon juice and capers.

Service is friendly, informal and efficient, and Divino regulars are on a first-name basis with the staff.

Enzo & Angela

013

Italian

11701 Wilshire Blvd. (at Barrington Ave.)

Phone:	310-477-3880	Mon – Fri lunch & dinner
Web:	www.enzoandangela.com	Sat – Sun dinner only
Prices:	**$$**	

The scarcity of interesting space in Los Angeles leaves many restaurateurs with site choices that don't measure up to their visions. Here again is a jewel tucked into a strip mall, just off Wilshire Boulevard. Inside, however, the bright dining room recalls a beachfront Adriatic hotel, in which white linens and seascape paintings buffer the tension of traffic and commerce. Excellent home-style dishes banish it altogether.

A house minestrone filled with al dente vegetables relies on the subtle taste of its ingredients. Artistic selections like *spigola con checca* (flaky Mediterranean sea bass layered with fresh, ripe, red tomatoes and herbs, and doused with lemon juice, white wine and capers) open a visceral connection to the Old Country.

Ford's Filling Station

014

Gastropub

9531 Culver Blvd. (at Washington Blvd.), Culver City

Phone:	310-202-1470	Mon – Sat lunch & dinner
Web:	www.fordsfillingstation.net	
Prices:	**$$**	

When Benjamin Ford opened his restaurant in Culver City in early 2006, the place garnered a lot of attention due to its chef's celebrity lineage (yes, Benjamin is Harrison Ford's son). Since then, crowds have continued to come to fill up on the seasonal gastropub fare, meaning food in the public-house tradition, but of far greater refinement.

This relaxed, wood-and-brick foodie hangout changes its menu with the daily market. While more ambitious dishes (whole brook trout laid atop a bed of sautéed broccolini and oyster mushrooms, surrounded by a bright green pool of scallion-infused olive oil and dollops of hazelnut cream) highlight the kitchen's expertise, the menu mainstays—particularly the terrific burger—are favorites with the regulars.

Fraîche

015

Mediterranean

9411 Culver Blvd. (bet. Cardiff Ave. & Main St.), Culver City

Phone:	310-839-6800	Tue – Fri lunch & dinner
Web:	www.fraicherestaurantla.com	Sat – Sun dinner only
Prices:	**$$**	

A fresh face in Culver City's burgeoning restaurant scene, this bistro's young kitchen staff brings considerable skill to its flavorful dishes. Appetizers run to things like beef tartare, charcuterie (think aged prosciutto), and a white gazpacho with roasted almonds and red grapes. Mediterranean inspiration is evident in a vegetable-laced lamb *spezzatino,* its bite-size pieces coated with a thick tomato-herb sauce reduced from the stewing liquid and served with herb-scented ricotta gnocchi. Pastas run the regional gamut from tortelli with braised rabbit to *fruits de mer,* brimming with shellfish.

Rich wood flooring, cushioned chairs, a casual front bar and an open kitchen all say "come in and relax." The casual-chic crowd seems happy to oblige.

French 75

016

French

10250 Santa Monica Blvd. (off Constellation Blvd.)

Phone:	310-788-0700	Lunch & dinner daily
Web:	www.french75bistro.com	
Prices:	**$$$**	

This lively bistro finds itself in Westfield Century City Mall, but it could just as easily be set on the *Rive Gauche* in Paris. No surprise, then, that the exceptional French onion soup *gratinée* is deeply flavorful, its Emmental cheese top perfectly caramelized; or that the Callebaut chocolate soufflé is fluffy and delightful, made only more so by the scoop of Cointreau-spiked whipped cream and the generous drizzle of dark-chocolate sauce that are added tableside.

The name refers to the 75mm cannon that helped drive Germany to the peace table in World War I, and to the Cognac and Champagne concoction that officers drank from the cannon's spent shell casings. The owners' affection for such detail is reflected in the authentic interior.

Hamasaku

 Japanese

017

11043 Santa Monica Blvd. (at S. Bentley Ave.)

Phone:	310-479-7636	Mon – Fri lunch & dinner
Web:	www.hamasakula.com	Sat dinner only
Prices:	$$$	

In LA, it seems, the only locations that matter are where movies are filmed. This tiny sushi house's setting, in a nondescript strip mall (but in a modern Japanese-style room), matters not at all to its celebrity-studded cadre of loyals. What does matter is the enduring buzz that its imaginative raw-fish offerings are among the best—market-fresh and expertly handled.

Many of the unique sushi rolls bear the names of the regulars who requested them. Lyon's Kids Roll, for example, wraps tender pieces of lobster in seasoned sushi rice with a thin layer of crisped rice on the outside. Friendly servers can answer questions about the arm's-length sushi list. Then off you go with your pencil and menu—but do first ask about the chef's *omakase* choices.

Hide Sushi

 Japanese

018

2040 Sawtelle Blvd. (bet. La Grange & Mississippi Aves.)

Phone:	310-477-7242	Tue – Sun lunch & dinner
Web:	N/A	
Prices:		

Couched amid authentic Japanese grocery and hardware stores, gift and magazine shops, nurseries and restaurants, this modestly decorated sushi and sashimi restaurant stands out above the competition on this stretch of Sawtelle Boulevard for pairing high-quality ingredients with notably low prices.

Cooked items are limited here. The memorable fare flows from the skill behind the ten-seat sushi bar, so if you stick with the raw-fish dishes, you won't be disappointed. Service is efficient, if a bit frantic; the restaurant seems to be always packed with local regulars who wait patiently for a seat.

Although Hide Sushi takes cash only, there's an ATM inside, just in case you forget. Parking is in the back lot, accessed by a narrow alley.

Il Grano

019

Italian

11359 Santa Monica Blvd. (bet. Corinth & Purdue Aves.)

Phone:	310-477-7886	Mon – Fri lunch & dinner
Web:	N/A	Sat dinner only
Prices:	$$$	

A recent makeover brightened up the décor of chef Sal Marino's creation to match his culinary panache. His signature *crudo* (raw fish served Italian-style, with light olive oil or a dash of fresh herbs) is a favorite of his fans, many of whom are recognized as regulars.

Playing on the seasons, the menu adds daily specials according to the quality of market products. The kitchen excels at seafood dishes and at marrying ingredients to display their natural flavors. Thus, a smooth soup made from the purée of fresh white carrots does not need cream to enrich it; a slice of melting burrata cheese, a simple drizzle of olive oil, and a sprinkle of chopped chives suffice. An extensive collection of Italian wines—some quite rare—dominates the wine list.

Il Moro

020

Italian

11400 W. Olympic Blvd. (at Purdue Ave.)

Phone:	310-575-3530	Mon – Fri lunch & dinner
Web:	www.ilmoro.com	Sat – Sun dinner only
Prices:	$$$	

You enter this highrise off a side street and walk through a modern bar/lounge to find a spacious, soaring room, beautifully appointed with floor-to-ceiling windows. Outdoor tables set in a palm-studded garden with a trickling stream enhance the restaurant's commercial setting.

Chef Davide Ghizzoni, who hails from Northern Italy, presided over Il Moro's debut in 1994, drawing inspiration from his native region. So, thin slices of shaved artichoke hearts on a bed of arugula are tossed in lemon juice and fruity olive oil, and capped with shaved aged parmesan. Roasted wild boar marries well with wide, flat ribbons of pappardelle pasta and a rich, tomato ragù flavored with garlic, onion and salty pecorino cheese. This is how it's done in Emilia Romagna.

Javan

021

Persian

11500 Santa Monica Blvd. (at Butler Ave.)

Phone: 310-207-5555   Lunch & dinner daily

Web: www.javanrestaurant.com

Prices: 💰

Prompt and attentive service, fresh quality ingredients, pride in Persian cuisine and a mastery of its techniques number among the strong points of this warmly lit dining room, which looks out on a busy commercial neighborhood. Naturally, you'll find many patrons from the local Persian community here, but the flavorful dishes have won it a wider audience.

Chicken *koobideh*, ground and seasoned with saffron and other spices, roasted on skewers over an open fire, then served with steamed basmati rice and a roasted tomato, is a close cousin to other meat dishes, particularly lamb and beef. Stews such as *fesenjun* (sautéed walnuts cooked in pomegranate sauce and mixed with chicken) and other specials are only offered on specific days of the week.

Kaizuka

022

Japanese

9729 Culver Blvd. (at Duquesne Ave.), Culver City

Phone: 310-253-5038   Mon – Fri lunch & dinner

Web: N/A   Sat dinner only

Prices: 💰

Facing City Hall from its shady sidewalk patio, this casual downtown cafe serves traditional sushi along with some hot entrées, all reasonably priced. The chef's combination lunch, an *omakase* menu, draw diners from nearby businesses, including industry types from the Sony Pictures complex on the old MGM Studios lot.

Order a bowl of edamame (soy bean pods cooked in salted water) to enjoy while you consider the sushi list. Be brave. Order the eel avocado roll. What arrives is a cut roll of tender pieces of smoky-sweet and salty roast eel, and creamy chunks of avocado. Here they make sushi rolls in a measured way, so accents like sliced scallion or red-chile paste don't overpower the natural flavors of the fish.

Katsuya

023

J a p a n e s e

11777 San Vicente Blvd. (bet. Gorham & Montana Aves.)

Phone:	310-207-8744	Mon – Fri lunch & dinner
Web:	www.sbeent.com/katsuya	Sat – Sun dinner only
Prices:	$$	

Philippe Starck designed it, which means you might feel as self-conscious as a runway model the first time you sashay through the door. Starck's trademark white surfaces, bright screens and candles are everywhere, while cushy sofas cozy up in the lounge. It's a see-and-be-seen Brentwood scene.

There are three kitchens for food, a fourth for "liquids." Out of the first three come simple statements like almond-crusted scallops or duck breast with yuzu pepper from the robata grill. A large, dried Hoba leaf holds a piece of black cod and the miso glaze in which it's cooked. There's also a wide selection of sushi and sashimi.

Chef Katsuya Uechi started his chain of LA restaurants with Sushi Katsu-ya in Studio City and Encino.

Kiriko

024

J a p a n e s e

11301 Olympic Blvd. (at Sawtelle Ave.)

Phone:	310-478-7769	Tue – Fri lunch & dinner
Web:	www.kirikosushi.com	Sat – Sun dinner only
Prices:		

Omakase selections are the high point of this homespun little place, where the rustic wood sushi bar and plain wooden chairs and tables account for décor. (There's also a traditional low table with cushions for four at the back of the long, narrow room.)

Though the menu offers raw fish and hot cooked dishes, the chefs' choice, drawing on the finest fish available at the market that day, delivers the best of what the kitchen can offer. Their sashimi picks may include tuna (probably *toro*, the fatty, most prized cut), halibut, mackerel, or salmon fanned over mounds of shaved daikon radish and sprinkled with a yuzu-scented ponzu sauce.

Parking is free in the underground garage of the Olympic Collection conference center where Kiriko is located.

K-Zo

025

Japanese ✗✗

9240 Culver Blvd. (at Venice Blvd.), Culver City

Phone:	310-202-8890	Mon – Fri lunch & dinner
Web:	www.k-zo.com	Sat dinner only
Prices:	$$	

Chef Keizo Ishiba, classically trained in Japan and France, injects European sensibilities into his sushi, sashimi and small plates, creating both traditional and contemporary flavors in his raw fish and hot food courses. The space is industrial, with concrete floors and big load-bearing columns softened by comfortable seating, wooden tables and bud vases. There's a sake bar in front, a sushi bar in back.

You'll see old and new fused in a *wakame* seaweed salad, an eye-pleasing arrangement of four other types of ocean greens with curling scallion spirals, some flavored with sesame oil and rice-wine vinegar. So, too, in baked lobster wrapped in soy paper with asparagus, caramelized mirin hollandaise and toasted sesame seeds. Word is spreading.

La Cachette

026

French ✗✗✗

10506 Little Santa Monica Blvd. (at Thayer Ave.)

Phone:	310-470-4992	Mon – Fri lunch & dinner
Web:	www.lacachetterestaurant.com	Sat – Sun dinner only
Prices:	$$$$	

This "hiding place" is well named. Tucked away off Santa Monica Boulevard, La Cachette's entrance is in the back of the restaurant, down a little alley (enter from the rear parking area). Inside, the formal dining room is elegantly old-fashioned, set about with banquettes of yellow patterned fabric, mirrored walls, fresh flower arrangements, and large tables. Hand-decorated china fits the Old World feel.

In the kitchen, technical expertise treats premium California ingredients with French flair, as in sautéed sweetbreads over a slightly creamed morel sauce, paired with two ravioli stuffed with minced beef. Save room for dessert; a rustic fruit tart, for example, fills flaky puff pastry with nutty frangipane and fresh apricot halves.

La Serenata Gourmet

027

Mexican

10924 W. Pico Blvd. (at Kelton Ave.)

Phone:	310-441-9667	Lunch & dinner daily
Web:	www.laserenataonline.com	
Prices:	💲💲	

Popular sister to La Serenata de Garibali, this restaurant's reputation for fresh, well-prepared food might mean a long wait for a table if you don't have a reservation. Once you're seated, a margarita and a bowl of crispy corn tortilla chips with spicy red salsa will settle you down pronto—either in one of the two main indoor dining rooms or on the small patio. In the former, exposed beams and wrought-iron fixtures impart a warm hacienda feel.

You could continue with a mahi mahi enchilada. The tender fish comes simply seasoned (just salt, pepper and lime juice) and tucked inside a flavorful corn tortilla, topped with melted Mexican cheese and a *salsa verde* redolent of garlic, lime and tomatillo.

There is metered parking on the street.

Literati II

028

Californian

12081 Wilshire Blvd. (at Bundy Dr.)

Phone:	310-479-3400	Lunch & dinner daily
Web:	www.literati2.com	
Prices:	$$	

Outside is downtown Brentwood traffic. Inside, neutral walls and framed black-and-white photographs calm things down. A covered garden-patio dining area with flower-filled pots and vases of blooms on each table takes it down another notch. Touches like a basket of artisan bread and a dish of eggplant and roasted bell-pepper tapenade make you feel welcome. This is a lovely place to enjoy a meal.

What does Californian mean here? Torn mint leaves and crunchy radish wedges accenting a salad of cantaloupe and cucumber atop young bibb lettuce; or a delightful toasted brioche sandwich of Dungeness crab salad and avocado slices, served with parsnip chips and grape-studded coleslaw. The short wine list is offered at dinner, but can be requested at lunch.

Monte Alban

029

Mexican ✗✗

11927 Santa Monica Blvd. (at Brockton Ave.)

Phone:	310-444-7736	Lunch & dinner daily
Web:	N/A	
Prices:	〄	

The owners' loyalty to Oaxacan specialties, using traditional ingredients, is such that their pungent flavors are not tempered for the American palate. Tiled floors, Oaxacan fabrics, and a blue-sky ceiling with painted clouds infuse the dining rooms with a beguiling South-of-the-Border feel.

So does a salad of pickled cactus-paddle strips, jalapeño and diced tomato. The restaurant's name, Spanish for "white mountain," echoes a pre-Columbian city occupied by the Zapotec civilization, and later by the Mixtec, so no wonder the thick *mole negro* ladled onto a roasted chicken breast combines a multidimensional mix of fragrant spices, smoky chocolate and zesty chiles. Just as genuine is *nicuatole*, Oaxacan flan spiked with freshly ground cinnamon.

Nanbankan

031

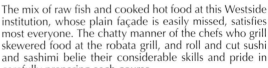

Japanese ✗

11330 Santa Monica Blvd. (at Corinth Ave.)

Phone:	310-478-1591	Dinner daily
Web:	N/A	
Prices:	〄	

The mix of raw fish and cooked hot food at this Westside institution, whose plain façade is easily missed, satisfies most everyone. The chatty manner of the chefs who grill skewered food at the robata grill, and roll and cut sushi and sashimi belie their considerable skills and pride in carefully preparing each course.

In addition to daily specials, there are rolls galore (as in spicy tuna pumped up with sesame oil and hot chile and wrapped with radish, bean sprouts, carrot and cucumber). The robata grill turns out skewers of eggplant or shiitake mushrooms, chicken or beef. To watch the chefs work close-up is most rewarding—especially when you see something unfamiliar that looks utterly delicious.

There's street parking, as well as a small rear lot.

Mori Sushi ✿

Japanese 🍴

11500 W. Pico Blvd. (at Gateway Blvd.)

Phone:	310-479-3939	Mon – Fri lunch & dinner
Web:	www.morisushi.org	Sat dinner only
Prices:	$$$	

Westside

Mori Sushi

A meal at Mori Sushi is an education into what excellent Japanese food should be. This, as chef/owner Morihiro Onodera asserts, is a sushi restaurant, serving only fish and vegetables. Whether you pencil orders on the sushi list, order small plates à la carte, or opt for the chef's *omakase*, what arrives will be sublime. Delicate slices of raw yellowtail are drizzled with fruity olive oil and soy sauce. Flavorful, smoky grilled barracuda comes atop a rectangle of sushi rice, with fresh wasabi grated in between.

Many of the *utsuwa* (serving plates) are handmade by Onodera and chef Hiroyuki Taniguchi, who believe that an appropriate serving vessel enhances a dish's flavor. They also recognize that Japanese sake goes best with sushi, and the extensive sake list reflects this. Even the simple wood chairs and uncovered tables bow to the primacy of food. Standards are set here.

Appetizers

- Mori's Homemade Tofu with Mori's Blend Soy Sauce and Fresh Wasabi
- *Nasu Dengaku*, Eggplant with two types of Miso
- *Osuimono*, Traditional Clear Soup

Entrées

- Sushi
- Abalone Tempura with Lemon and various Sea Salts
- *Yumegokochi* Rice exclusively cultivated for Mori Sushi

Desserts

- *Yokan*, Homemade Jelly Cake in Red Bean or Persimmon
- Homemade Ice Cream in Sesame or Pumpkin
- Seasonal Fresh Japanese *Totti* Pear or White Peach

Napa Valley Grille

032

1100 Glendon Ave. (at Lindbrook Dr.)

Phone: 310-824-3322   Lunch & dinner daily
Web: www.napavalleygrille.com
Prices: $$$

California's northern and southern halves are so distinct there's always talk of dividing the Golden State in two. No need. This grill brings a taste of the northern Wine Country to Westwood with its fresh California produce and Napa wines. Even the outdoor patio makes a heroic effort to emulate the bucolic gardens found at Napa's most hospitable wineries.

Italians played an important role in the Wine Country's development, and the menu pays this homage. So, heirloom tomato bruschetta means grilled sourdough with minced fresh garlic, basil and olive oil, while artichoke ravioli topped with herbed tomato sauce, shredded parmesan and kalamata olives crosses the Bear Flag with the *Tricolore*.

There's even a late-hour bar menu for night owls.

Native Foods

033

1110 1/2 Gayley Ave. (at Lindbrook Dr.)

Phone: 310-209-1055   Lunch & dinner daily
Web: www.nativefoods.com
Prices:

It may be tiny, but this hole-in-the-wall dishes up some big beliefs, beginning with promoting a balanced, nutritious diet that doesn't include animal products. Native Foods takes vegan cuisine to heart, substituting grilled tempeh (soybean in cake form) for chicken in satays (called Thai sticks on the menu) served with a tasty peanut dipping sauce. Playing the part of fish, tempeh joins shredded cabbage, tomato salsa and guacamole inside a grilled corn tortilla billed as a "Baja surf taco." It all works well.

Place your order and pay at the cash register, then squeeze past the bins of veggies and fruit as you make your way upstairs to the small balcony to eat. From here you'll have a bird's-eye view of the efficient staff in the open kitchen.

Nizam of India

Indian ✕✕

10871 W. Pico Blvd. (at Westwood Blvd.)

Phone: 310-470-1441   Lunch & dinner daily
Web: N/A
Prices:

   Authentic food and gracious service compensate for the dated décor in this storefront enterprise. The food here is fresh, simple, delicately spiced and delicious.

You'll find traditional items like grilled naan, a flatbread ubiquitous on Indian tables, flavored with toasted black sesame and caraway seeds, caramelized outside and chewy and airy within. Another classic, *dal papri* (small, fried lentil-flour crisps) is served with thin, cold slices of boiled potato, small pieces of raw white onion, and cilantro leaves, the mixture dolloped with cool yogurt and dusted with spices. Indians see *chana peshawari* as comfort food, and no wonder. Its creamy stewed chickpeas are cooked with ginger, garlic and cumin, and garnished with fresh cilantro.

Nook Bistro

Contemporary ✕✕

11628 Santa Monica Blvd. (at Barry Ave.)

Phone: 310-207-5160   Mon – Fri lunch & dinner
Web: www.nookbistro.com   Sat dinner only
Prices: $$

   True to its name, this modern bistro hides in the corner of a strip mall off busy Santa Monica Boulevard. The sleek interior, with its stained and polished concrete floors, exposed ductwork, and Postmodern furnishings, could be in a New York loft. Could be, but it's in West LA.

Young, black-clad servers gladly offer recommendations about the menu, where every unpretentious course displays culinary skill, winning flavor combinations and attention to detail. Pieces of poblano chile add smoky heat to a velvety yam soup. Smothered on the roasted red potatoes and fresh *haricots vert* that accompany a tender grilled flatiron steak, truffled crème fraîche contributes a pleasing richness to the meat. Desserts are in the same league.

Orris

036

Fusion ✕✕

2006 Sawtelle Blvd. (at La Grange Ave.)

Phone:	310-268-2212	Tue – Sun dinner only
Web:	www.orrisrestaurant.com	
Prices:	$$	

Clearly the focal point in this fun, hip dining room is the long exhibition kitchen, source of the "world cuisine" tapas on the constantly changing menu. The décor is sleek and simple with standard flatware and bright placemats injecting blasts of vivid color. Orchids at the bar and votive candles here and there add a soft elegance.

Chef Hideo Yamashiro's view is that the best cuisine is found, collectively, at all points of the compass. So don't try to trace the origin of red snapper carpaccio, which here is lightly browned, accented with olive oil, a bit of ginger and a bit of lime zest. Halibut tempura sounds Japanese, but in a pool of chunky pomodoro sauce, seasoned with fresh, woodsy rosemary and spicy oregano, all bets are off.

Osteria Latini

037

Italian ✕✕

11712 San Vicente Blvd. (at Barrington Ave.)

Phone:	310-826-9222	Mon – Fri lunch & dinner
Web:	www.osterialatini.com	Sat – Sun dinner only
Prices:	$$	

Come evening, chef/owner Paolo Pasio works the tables, greeting regulars and pitching specials like suckling pig, osso buco, and calamari stuffed with lump crabmeat. His first-name familiarity creates a convivial air, as does the dining room, decorated with greenery, rosewood floors, and wine-storage racks that double as partitions.

Born in Trieste, Pasio worked his way to the City of Angels, where he now oversees the skilled crew and top-flight ingredients that rule this kitchen. You taste his talent in a creamy roasted mushroom soup made without dairy, or a bowl of al dente bombolotti pasta tossed in an herbed tomato sauce and deliciously paired with roasted chicken breast. The wine list features a wide-ranging collection of Italian labels.

Palmeri Ristorante

038 Italian

11650 San Vicente Blvd. (at Bringham Ave.)

Phone:	310-442-8446	Mon – Sat lunch & dinner
Web:	N/A	Sun dinner only
Prices:	**$$$**	

Choose Palmeri among the handful of Italian restaurants you'll find within a four-block radius of the corner of San Vicente Boulevard and Barrington Avenue. In this plain modern room, where marble floors and maple wainscoting set off Italian glass chandeliers, high-quality Californian and Italian ingredients are melded together to create elegant dishes.

A selection of two signature dishes, the *piatto unico* showcases the likes of squid-ink ravioli filled with sweet crabmeat in a delicate, saffron-infused cream sauce. The combination may also include meaty prawns shelled and wrapped in a thin layer of swordfish and fresh oregano to keep the fish moist.

The waitstaff is attentive and prompt, and you'll find parking behind the restaurant.

Pecorino

039 Italian

11604 San Vicente Blvd. (bet. Bringham & Mayfield Aves.)

Phone:	310-571-3800	Mon – Fri lunch & dinner
Web:	www.pecorinorestaurant.com	Sat – Sun dinner only
Prices:	**$$$**	

In this European-style charmer, where a working trio of partners chatters in Italian, authentic home-style food is served in generous portions. Daily specials reflect the best from seasonal harvests; thus, in fall, green asparagus may come covered with a fontina cheese gratin and shaved black truffle. The chefs' rural sentiments are apparent in an Ahi tuna steak seared in olive oil, sliced, fanned over scallion-infused mashed potatoes and topped with a thick, chunky sauce of roasted cherry tomatoes, whole green peppercorns, sliced scallions and olive oil. Ever vigilant, one of the partners checks each plate before it leaves the kitchen.

Brick walls, exposed ceiling beams, wrought-iron light fixtures and an open kitchen boost the rustic vibe.

Pizzicotto

 Italian

040

11758 San Vicente Blvd. (at Barrington Ave.)

Phone:	310-442-7188	Mon – Sat lunch & dinner
Web:	N/A	Sun dinner only
Prices:	$$	

 Known primarily for traditional pizza, this self-described "Italian market bistro" promotes that feel with its display of Italian food products, and the braids of garlic and clusters of dried chile peppers that hang over the service counter.

The open kitchen can spin a mean pizza, but also start you out with little joys like an aged prosciutto di Parma, topped with earthy truffled honey. Sprinkle cantaloupe melon balls, fresh fig quarters, and a chiffonade of fresh basil on this and you sense the repertoire here goes well beyond pies. Even so, the pizzas *are* terrific, with thin crusts and crispy edges, finely seasoned sauces, fresh everything and lots of it.

For dessert, the likes of a lusciously moist lemon pine-nut cake hits the sweet spot.

Restaurant at the Getty Center

Californian

041

1200 Getty Center Dr. (off Sepulveda Blvd.)

Phone:	310-440-6810	Tue – Thu, Sun lunch only
Web:	www.getty.edu	Fri – Sat lunch & dinner
Prices:	$$$	

 Perched on a hilltop overlooking Los Angeles and the Pacific Ocean, the architecturally stunning Getty Center is a must-see on any visitor's list. The experience of wandering the museum's galleries is only enhanced by a lunch or a weekend sunset dinner at the restaurant. With its lofty skylit ceilings and glass walls flooding the minimalist space with changing light, the restaurant boasts sublime views from inside or out on the terrace.

Californian cuisine encompasses a world of possibilities. You see a sampling of these on the weekly changing menu, say, in an autumn heirloom-squash salad tossed with dates, aged Jack cheese, and toasted pumpkin seeds in a brown-butter vinaigrette.

Reservations are recommended. Park in the Center's garage.

Saketini

042   Asian

150 S. Barrington Ave. (at S. Barrington Pl.)

Phone:	310-440-5553	Mon – Fri lunch & dinner
Web:	www.saketini.com	Sat – Sun dinner only
Prices:	$$	

There are only seven tables in this quaint neighborhood gem, whimsically decorated with children's drawings, Asian wall hangings and bright seat cushions. Sushi represents Japan, while selections like *bulgogi* (strips of beef marinated in soy sauce, dark sesame oil, spring onions and garlic) add a taste of Korea. Nods to other Asian cuisines produce combinations like a salad of baby greens topped with strings of raw carrot in a ginger vinaigrette. This is served with a piece of silken tofu covered with a light tempura batter and fried to a golden brown, then drizzled with a reduction of syrupy, sweet soy sauce.

A small sidewalk patio for dining and free validated parking in a nearby lot makes this a relaxing, easy-to-reach destination.

Shaherzad

043   Persian

1422 Westwood Blvd. (at Wilkins Ave.)

Phone:	310-470-3242	Lunch & dinner daily
Web:	N/A	
Prices:		

Not mere Persian cuisine, proclaims the neon outside, but "royal" Persian cuisine. That must strike a harmonious chord in the Westside's Iranian-American community, for this longtime Westwood favorite is usually thronged with Farsi speakers, many arriving arm-in-arm from nearby neighborhoods.

From the bricks of the traditional *tanour* oven come baskets of slightly charred *tanouri* flatbread, served to you promptly upon being seated. This is a traditional place, that makes liberal use of cardamom, rosewater and saffron, the last mixed with yogurt and fragrant basmati rice into casserole-style *tahchin* with a layer of tender shredded chicken in the center. Portions are large, requiring willpower to save room for dessert. If you do, the reward is a plate of delicious baklava.

Sushi Sasabune

044

12400 Wilshire Blvd. (bet. Carmelina Ave. & McClellan Dr.)

Phone: 310-820-3596   Mon – Fri lunch & dinner
Web: N/A
Prices: **$$$**

Located in a bustling Wilshire business district, on the ground floor of a large office building, this no-frills enterprise hews to traditional flavor combinations using fresh, premium-quality fish for its sushi, sashimi and grilled fish dishes.

A small team of chefs work behind the big U-shaped sushi bar, rolling and chopping, fanning thin slices of raw albacore in a mixture of tangy soy sauce and rice-wine vinegar, and sprinkling them with slices of sharp scallion. Using warm sweetened sushi rice, they offer a chef's assortment, some garnished with smoked-eel sauce, others with a citrus-infused ponzu, soy and vinegar sauce or pickled daikon radish.

Street parking is scarce, but you can use the building's underground garage.

Taiko

045

11677 San Vicente Blvd. (at Barrington Ave.)

Phone: 310-207-7782   Lunch & dinner daily
Web: N/A
Prices:

Located on the top level of a Brentwood shopping complex, this casual-yet-contemporary noodle shop offers generous portions of modestly priced fare. The menu showcases steaming bowls of soba (buckwheat) and udon (white wheat) noodles afloat in fragrant fish broths. You can fill your bowl, item by item, with seaweed, bean curd, mountain vegetables, mushrooms, seafood and meats.

There is excellent sushi and sashimi, too, and *donburi* bowls (sushi rice topped with your choice of add-ons) come with miso soup and salad. Hot entrées range from prime rib to tuna filet mignon and broiled Chilean sea bass *Kasuzuke*, the latter marinated in a sake-miso paste. Expect good ingredients, good service, and a very affordable Bento box lunch special.

Westside

Takao

 Japanese

046

11656 San Vicente Blvd. (at Darlington Ave.)

Phone: 310-207-8636 Mon – Sat lunch & dinner
Web: N/A Sun dinner only
Prices: $$

What Takao's plain black tile floors and taupe walls lack in eye appeal is made up for with warm service and fresh, simple, high-quality fare. Sushi and sashimi get top billing in the small L-shaped dining room and at the sushi bar, but cooked dishes are also offered.

On weekdays, the popular business lunch might be a deluxe sushi sampler with a California roll of crab and avocado, along with raw tuna, yellowtail, white fish, salmon, prawns and red snapper. Check the board for daily specials, featured seasonal ingredients, and the chef's latest inspirations. Chef/owner Takao is a fixture behind the counter, overseeing the preparation of his straightforward food.

The busy street makes self-parking problematic; let a valet handle it.

Tengu

 Japanese

047

10853 Lindbrook Dr. (at Hilgard Ave.)

Phone: 310-209-0071 Mon – Fri lunch & dinner
Web: www.tengu.com Sat – Sun dinner only
Prices: $$

Enter off a small courtyard into a gray multilevel dining room crowded with rosewood-colored tables, and a sushi bar illuminated by decorative drop lights and backlit Japanese screens. This Westwood Village hipster draws local business types at lunch; some evenings, a DJ spins groove music.

You'll find playful items like Samango, a roll of salmon, crab, mango, smelt roe and wasabi cream. More innovative are sake-fired garlic sprouts, a layered Asian tartare, and baby yellowtail carpaccio with chives and truffle oil. Surpassing the usual, the dessert menu offers intriguing options like sweet and crispy banana tempura balanced by spicy ginger ice cream.

If you're in Santa Monica, check out Tengu's new location at 1541 Ocean Avenue.

 Westside

189

Tlapazola Grill

048

11676 Gateway Blvd. (at Barrington Ave.)

Phone:	310-477-1577	Tue – Sat lunch & dinner
Web:	N/A	Mon & Sun dinner only
Prices:	**$$**	

Uninspiring as most are, LA's strip malls offer restaurateurs a place to start, with a few free parking spaces thrown in. This grill's owners use traditional dance masks and whimsical paintings to transform their dining room into an appealing salute to their native Oaxaca.
That requires classic dishes like *carne asada* (a ribeye steak), grilled trout tacos, *barbacoa de borrego* (braised lamb), masa pancakes with smoky achiote shrimp, and a nopalitos-cactus salad. Chalk up the lobster enchiladas to native inspiration, and trust the friendly waitstaff to explain the many daily specials.
If you're a tequila fan, be sure to sample the extensive collection of tequilas, either here or at the second location on Lincoln Boulevard in Marina del Rey.

Torafuku

049

10914 Pico Blvd. (bet. Veteran Ave. & Westwood Blvd.)

Phone:	310-470-0014	Mon – Sat lunch & dinner
Web:	www.torafuku-usa.com	Sun dinner only
Prices:	**$$**	

Delicious, authentic food accounts for Torafuku's mostly Japanese clientele, who line its large square tables and exhibition kitchen. Traditional techniques paired with authentic ingredients result in classic home-style dishes.
This is the first US outpost of a small Japanese chain known for its centuries-old *kamado* method of cooking rice, one requiring a 500-pound iron pot placed in a stone and earthenware oven in order to create a unique consistency and flavor profile. Torafuku's homemade tofu, served in the bamboo container it is steamed in, is silky and slightly nutty. Sushi and sashimi share the menu with various cooked dishes, and a sake list runs the gamut from honey overtones to hints of pear, melon or apple.

Westside

2117

050

2117 Sawtelle Blvd. (at Mississippi Ave.)

Phone:	310-477-1617	Tue – Sat lunch & dinner
Web:	N/A	Sun dinner only
Prices:	$$	

Organic ingredients rule in this sophisticated melding of the cuisines of Europe, Asia and California. Dad cooks, Mom manages the dining room, and their daughter is lead server. The covered and screened front terrace offers an alternative to the small dining room.

Appetizers include things like roasted Chinese duck egg rolls in a pool of Mandarin orange sauce, sautéed sweetbreads, or a layered crab salad with a smear of pungent wasabi. Fusion being a culinary license to globe-trot, you may find lamb Wellington with black-truffle sauce, a roasted Kurobuta pork loin stuffed with goat cheese and dried grapes, or even a crispy soft-shell crab with risotto.

Parking is limited in this strip-mall location, but valet service eases any stress.

Vincenti Ristorante

051

11930 San Vicente Blvd. (at Montana Ave.)

Phone:	310-207-0127	Mon – Thu & Sat dinner only
Web:	www.vincentiristorante.com	Fri lunch & dinner
Prices:	$$$$	

Locals come to this Brentwood spot for romantic candlelight dinners, most dressing on a par with the upscale décor that encompasses Scandinavian wood floors, leather banquettes, and graceful, suspended light fixtures. A glass wall showcases the kitchen, and a wood-burning rotisserie juts into the dining room, tantalizing diners with its display of roasting meat.

Perhaps the most popular menu option, a long list of nightly specials (a salad of finely sliced baby artichokes and shavings of parmesan atop a bed of arugula; green pappardelle with duck ragù) augments delightful combinations like pizza topped with zucchini flowers and fresh porcini mushrooms. The chef's six-course daily special eliminates the need to make difficult choices.

Westside

Wilson

International ✗

052

8631 Washington Blvd. (at Sherbourne Dr.), Culver City

Phone: 310-287-2093 Mon – Fri lunch & dinner
Web: www.wilsonfoodandwine.com Sat dinner only
Prices: **$$**

Behind the arresting concrete checkerboard façade of Culver City's Museum of Design Art and Architecture (MODAA), you'll discover thought-provoking exhibitions that explore the interstices where art and design meet. But that's not all. Stick around to taste the internationally inspired dishes served at Wilson, on the museum's ground floor.

Like the museum, the food is eclectic, the flavors bold. Choose a seat on the back patio and dig into a grilled and raw asparagus salad with truffled beet tartare, a rabbit Sloppy Joe, tagliolini carbonara with prosciutto, or a BLET—a bacon, lettuce and tomato sandwich updated with barbecued eel and garlic aïoli. Lunchtime attracts an entertainment-industry crowd, while dinner brings in local residents.

Zip Fusion

Asian ✗✗

053

11301 W. Olympic Blvd. (at Sawtelle Blvd.)

Phone: 310-575-3636 Mon – Fri lunch & dinner
Web: www.zipfusion.com Sat – Sun dinner only
Prices: **$$**

This stylish venue (and its downtown sibling at 744 E. Third St.) focuses on artful Korean and Japanese dishes rendered with fine California ingredients. Billed as the "Zip Incredible Salad," thin slices of marinated grilled beef are served on mixed greens dressed in a salty-sweet sesame-oil-based vinaigrette. Innovative "rolls" include the Whiskey & Soda, made without rice; and the Yahoo, topped with sliced jalapeños.

Black-cushioned metal lounge chairs, dark floors and indirect lighting create a hip ambience inside the restaurant, whose name (Zip) is Korean for "home." Many favor the stone patio, where potted palms and lush plantings evoke the tropics. Either way, expect a young crowd, electronic music, and happy hours devoted to karaoke and sushi.

innovation has good prospects whenever it is cleaner, safer and more efficient.

The MICHELIN Energy green tire lasts 25% longer*.
It also provides fuel savings of 2 to 3%
while reducing CO_2 emissions.

* on average compared to competing tires in the same category.

MICHELIN
A better way forward

Where to **stay**

Alphabetical list of Hotels

Where to **stay**

Avalon

001

9400 W. Olympic Blvd. (at Cañon Dr.)

Phone: 310-277-5221 or 800-535-4715
Fax: 310-277-4928
Web: www.avalonbeverlyhills.com
Prices: $$$

84
Rooms
4
Suites

Avalon Hotel

The relaxed "patio lifestyle" of mid-20th-century Southern California is the theme of the Avalon's homage to chic design from then to now. Three distinctive buildings dating from 1949 (now thoroughly updated) cluster in a quiet residential area near fine art galleries, high-end boutiques and A-list dining.

The main Olympic building, with 43 rooms and suites, hosts the hourglass pool, a fitness center, and a poolside restaurant—blue on blue—offering California fare and weekend brunch. Neighborhood views abound from the taller Beverly building's 26 rooms and 2 studio penthouses. Screenwriters in residence might prefer one of the 8 with kitchenettes in the 15-room Cañon, 4 with private patios. (Two villas are available for monthly rental.) Most rooms have balconies. Details like George Nelson lamps, Isamu Noguchi tables, Charles Eames-inspired chairs and Italian linens add beauty and comfort. Movie and music players are state-of-the-art.

Service is attentive and fast, valet parking organized and friendly. Of course, the Avalon is totally connected, with DSL and wireless, which means you can send script revisions even from the discreetly tented poolside cabanas.

Beverly Hills

Hotel Bel-Air

701 Stone Canyon Rd. (off Sunset Blvd.)

Phone: 310-472-1211 or 800-648-4097
Fax: 310-476-5890
Web: www.hotelbelair.com
Prices: $$$$

152 Rooms
39 Suites

Hotel Bel-Air

Nearly hidden by trees and meticulously groomed gardens, the Bel-Air sits on a dozen acres in a narrow canyon. What you glimpse as you enter suggests a Spanish Colonial estate. Cross the stone bridge over the swan-filled pond to the reception cottage and you enter an inviting maze of flower-lined brick paths and columned arcades. Turn a corner and there's an expansive oval pool flanked by teak lounges and curtained cabanas. Walk on and there's an outdoor dining terrace, a fitness center, another garden.

Of the property's 91 spacious guestrooms, more than a third are suites. Soon after you're in your room, which feels like a hideaway, a tea service arrives along with fresh fruit and a small pastry. Shortly after comes another knock to check that all's in order, offer ice for the mini-bar or light your fireplace.

The décor and furnishings are classically grand, stopping tastefully short of grandiose. Fabrics and linens are the finest, the bathrooms cozy and sumptuous. Come evening, you can dress up a bit and stroll back down that path to The Restaurant at Hotel Bel-Air *(see restaurant listing)*, where there's live music in the clubby lounge, and dining inside and out.

Beverly Hills

The Beverly Hills
Hotel & Bungalows

9641 Sunset Blvd. (at Crescent Dr.)

Phone: 310-276-2251 or 800-283-8885
Fax: 310-887-2887
Web: www.thebeverlyhillshotel.com
Prices: $$$$

145 Rooms

59 Suites

The Beverly Hills Hotel

On the slope of the wealthiest heights in zip code 90210, surrounded by estates and an air of supremacy among the city's most luxurious hotels, this palmy pink palace and its tropical gardens shelter a 12-acre world of ease. A thick red carpet runs from the porte-cochere valet-parking area into a palatial circular lobby with gilded pink armchairs, pale green sofas and the signature pink-and-green carpet. (The palm leaf is a recurring motif.) Winding paths lead through a manicured jungle to the 22 private bungalows—what tales they could tell!—to the fabled pool lined by lounges and cabanas, and lighted tennis courts.

Guestrooms, some with private patios, are spacious and elegantly old-fashioned. Beige carpets, downy bedcovers, swoopy curtains, and wood furniture leave no doubt that these rooms are primarily for leisure. Still, there is a spacious desk, a fax machine and high-speed Internet access. Bathrooms feature a jetted soaking tub with shower, plush linens and mats, and a separate toilet room. Service matches the promise of all this. The Polo Lounge *(see restaurant listing)* offers live music and fine dining inside as well as on the garden terrace.

Beverly Hilton

9876 Wilshire Blvd. (at Santa Monica Blvd.)

Phone:	310-274-7777
Fax:	310-285-1313
Web:	www.beverlyhilton.com
Prices:	$$$

469 Rooms

101 Suites

The Beverly Hilton

Lucy and Desi were in their heyday when this 570-room landmark opened a short stroll from Rodeo Drive. Nine of the 101 suites are luxury penthouses, party central during the Golden Globe Awards and other recurring events that fill up the three ballrooms here.

A recent $80-million makeover enhanced the iconic hotel's half-century of good will by adding contemporary luxury, moving the beloved but dated Trader Vic's Restaurant to the pool area where it reopened as Trader Vic's Lounge, and unveiling nearby Circa 55, a pricey morning-to-night venue featuring American cuisine.

Guestrooms in the Wilshire Tower overlook the boulevard. Poolside cabana rooms open out onto the pool deck or balconies above. Oasis rooms offer more privacy and quiet. All are spacious, with neutral earth tones intended to foster tranquility. The furniture is contemporary and functional; chairs match the height of desks large enough for serious work. Bathrooms feature cushy linens, high-end toiletries, large counters, roomy showers, and separate alcoves for the loo. White Frette linens, down comforters, bedside Bose stereos and a big-screen plasma TV make turning in early an attractive option.

Beverly Hills

Beverly Wilshire

005

9500 Wilshire Blvd. (at Rodeo Dr.)

Phone:	310-275-5200 or 800-332-3442
Fax:	310-275-5986
Web:	www.fourseasons.com
Prices:	$$$$

254
Rooms

141
Suites

Beverly Wilshire/Four Seasons

Its imposing Italian Renaissance height and iron-gated auto entrance off El Camino Drive suggest officialdom within. There is indeed an official air about the place, especially when flagstaffs along its Wilshire Boulevard façade display the colors of foreign nations. If downtown Beverly Hills has a Ministry of Shopping and Pampering, this is it.

Arriving by car, you enter the lobby from valet parking between the front Wilshire wing and the rear Beverly wing. Some rooms are a bit sedate, some perhaps a trifle small (the hotel was completed in 1928), and the pool is more suited to dipping than swimming laps, but there is no stinting on amenities. Quiet beige-carpeted hallways lead to guestrooms with cushioned chairs, table desks, feather beds, marble baths with tubs and separate showers and ample counter space. Plush terry robes and slippers wait in the closet.

The rear Beverly Wing houses a well-equipped fitness center and a full-service spa with an A-list clientele. You needn't venture outside for excellent food and people-watching. Wolfgang Puck's steakhouse Cut *(see restaurant listing)* and The Blvd *(see restaurant listing)* are located in the front Wilshire Wing.

Four Seasons Los Angeles at Beverly Hills

006

300 S. Doheny Dr. (bet Burton Way & 3rd St.)

Phone: 310-273-2222 or 800-332-3442
Fax: 310-385-4927
Web: www.fourseasons.com
Prices: $$$$

187
Rooms

98
Suites

Four Seasons

Far from Beverly Hills' see-and-be-seen hustle, among apartment houses and homes, this European-style hotel attracts people who see such separation as a plus. A circular drive from the palm-lined street lands you among bellmen who usher you into a lobby with an inlaid marble floor and vases of fresh flowers. Then it's upstairs and along thickly carpeted hallways to elegantly appointed guestrooms with classically inspired birch-tone furnishings.

You can cocoon here, spinning CDs and watching movies, emailing friends over a high-speed connection at a marble-topped desk, losing yourself in a book while plopped into a cushy armchair in the hotel's plush terry robe and slippers, or soaking in the tub in the beige marble bathroom. At bedtime comes turn-down service, followed by a dive under a down comforter.

You can be just as happily indolent outdoors by the big pool, in a cabana if you want more privacy than the potted greenery provides. Either way, towel and drink attendants will find you. On the fourth floor there's a well-equipped fitness center and a full-service spa.

Just off the lobby, Gardens *(see restaurant listing)* serves delicious contemporary fare.

Beverly Hills

Maison 140

007

140 Lasky Dr. (bet. Charleville & Wilshire blvds.)

Phone:	310-281-4000 or 866-891-0945
Fax:	310-281-4001
Web:	www.maison140beverlyhills.com
Prices:	$$

43
Rooms

Kor Hotel Group

Silent-film star Lillian Gish once owned this 1939 building, transformed by Kelly Wearstler (designer of the nearby Avalon, another Kor Hotel Group creation) into a hip amalgam of Chinoiserie with lots of red, black and gray accents. Touches drawn from the Jazz Age and Seventies Modernism conjure up the ambience of a Left Bank Parisian inn with a pronounced Far Eastern flavor.

Mandarin rooms span 300 square feet, Parisian rooms are smaller (200 square feet), but all share amenities. Here this means dormers, potted topiaries and red-lacquered doors, one-of-a-kind antiques, original commissioned artwork, customized furniture and fabrics, down comforters, Italian linens and terrycloth robes, in-room spa services, and pool privileges at the Avalon. Flat-screen TVs and CD/DVD players are at hand, of course, along with Internet connections and two-line phones. A fitness room with free weights and cardiovascular equipment is open 24/7. You park your car in a pay lot on the premises.

Downtown Beverly Hills is around the corner, but the hotel's lounge Bar Noir holds its own as a nightspot, and also hosts a self-serve breakfast to guests from early to mid-morning.

Beverly Hills

Mosaic

008

125 S. Spalding Dr. (off Wilshire Blvd.)

Phone:	310-278-0303 or 800-463-4466
Fax:	310-278-1728
Web:	www.mosaichotel.com
Prices:	$$$

44
Rooms

5
Suites

Mosaic

The lobby of this well-located four-story establishment is small, but the 49 rooms and suites on its upper three levels are large, quiet and pleasingly decorated in a contemporary European motif of earthy browns, mossy greens, heather and beige. Botanical prints and an occasional potted orchid, feather beds and bedding, plush carpets, a large overstuffed ottoman and shaded lamps offer the comforts of a cozy pied-à-terre. Windows open onto a tree-shaded courtyard or a residential street. One- and two-bedroom suites have 42-inch plasma TV screens, DVD players and oversized glass-enclosed showers.

Mosaic panels and partitions accent the common areas. Blacks and browns dominate small, chic Tastes restaurant, which serves regional European fare. Its French doors open onto the courtyard and a heated lap pool.

Well-trained and professional, the youthful staff dresses casually in Beverly Hills style. There's a day spa, and a state-of-the-art gym with free weights and a variety of exercise machines. Business travelers will appreciate high-speed in-room Internet connections, commodious desks, cordless phones and a lobby office printer accessible to guests.

Beverly Hills

The Peninsula

9882 South Santa Monica Blvd. (at Wilshire Blvd.)

Phone:	310-551-2888 or 800-462-7899
Fax:	310-788-2319
Web:	www.peninsula.com
Prices:	**$$$$**

160
Rooms

36
Suites

The Peninsula Beverly Hills

Given its amenities, including a rooftop spa and a pool with private cabanas, nightly live entertainment and the popular Belvedere *(see restaurant listing)*, this hotel could have been claimed by the young club-hopping Hollywood crowd that fancies itself uniquely qualified to judge everything. Somehow, it escaped that distinction, winning a following among wealthy professionals and leisure guests.

Sixteen of its 196 rooms are private villas, 36 are suites. All are spacious and appointed in classic European style, with ecru walls, crown moldings, canopied feather beds, and carved wooden nightstands matching the headboard and entertainment armoire. For serious work, there's a desk and a fax machine; a sitting area, a mini-bar and a wide, flat-screen television foster relaxation when the work is done.

Spacious baths of beige and rose marble include a soaking tub and a separate shower, as well as ample counter space. You'll appreciate thoughtful touches like Molton Brown bath products, high-quality towels and linens, and a comfy bathrobe and slippers. At night a warming fireplace adds romantic magic to the casual Roof Garden cafe.

Beverly Hills

Raffles L'Ermitage

9291 Burton Way (bet Foothill Rd. & Maple Dr.)

Phone: 310-278-3344 or 800-800-2113
Fax: 310-278-8247
Web: www.raffles-lermitagehotel.com
Prices: $$$$

103 Rooms

16 Suites

Raffles L'Ermitage Beverly Hills

Proclaiming itself a "sanctuary," Raffles strikes a chord with people who count privacy among the luxuries that separate good hotels from great ones. Details include a private entrance for those wishing to avoid the public eye, and elevators accessible only with a room key. That means no paparazzi on the rooftop sun deck and pool area, or in the fitness center, and all room service preceded by a call.

Service sets the bar high at this tranquil Euro-Asian hotel, yet the atmosphere is subdued—designed around soothing neutral tones. Off the lobby, Jaan restaurant features a lush patio in addition to its domed, gold-and-white dining room.

Spacious rooms reflect the East-West duality in the light-toned, polished-wood panels, and the beige carpets, walls and linens that create a spa-like serenity. All guest quarters have private balconies. King-size feather beds are set low in the Japanese style; you control the lights from a bedside panel. Plush armchairs with a footrest offer a place to read or watch the big-screen TV. Marble bathrooms are unstinting, with a soaking tub, a separate shower, a double sink, and a walk-in closet with dressing room. Yes, this is how stars live.

Beverly Hills

205

Omni

251 S. Olive St. (bet. 2nd & 3rd Sts.)

Phone:	213-617-3300 or 888-444-6664
Fax:	213-617-3399
Web:	www.omnihotels.com
Prices:	$$

453
Rooms

Omni Hotels

When young novelist John Fante, who is to Los Angeles what James Joyce is to Dublin, checked into the Alta Vista hotel on Bunker Hill during the Depression years it was a down-at-the-heels bump on the Downtown landscape. Everything has changed, including the hill itself, crew-cut long ago for highrises like the Wells Fargo Center. Where Fante and his fictional alter-ego Arturo Bandini wandered hungry, the Museum of Contemporary Art now stands. On the far side of the block next to the Walt Disney Hall is this 453-room, 17-story tower, where today's Downtown literati order martinis and cigars at Noé *(see restaurant listing)*.

The business of Downtown is mostly business, and the Omni efficiently caters to commercial travelers, with spacious, impeccably clean rooms, a business center, dozens of meeting-room configurations, a spa, and a fitness center and outdoor lap pool to work out the kinks from sitting all day.

The Dorothy Chandler Pavilion, home to the Los Angeles Philharmonic and the Los Angeles Symphony, is two blocks away in the same complex as the city's premiere theatrical venue, the Mark Taper Forum and Ahmanson Theater. This is a quiet, safe area at night.

Standard Downtown

550 S. Flower St. (at 6th St.)

Phone:	213-892-8080
Fax:	213-623-4455
Web:	www.standardhotel.com
Prices:	**$$**

205
Rooms

2
Suites

The Standard

Back when Elvis was still in high school, the Superior Oil company's owners asked Claud Beelman to design a headquarters building celebrating the technological advancement of the age. They got it. Beelman's Modernist vision, finished in 1956, is an archetype of mid-century Californian architecture. Now part of a hotel, the building's lobby is a designated landmark.

These days, mercantile ambition is a fading ghost here. Downtown LA's revitalization is led less by corporate captains than by those working Beelman's side of the street: designers, artists, media entrepreneurs, writers, filmmakers and others attracted by the availability of big spaces like those in the Standard.

This is a fun hotel, with large rooms, retro furnishings and décor, a 24-hour restaurant, a fitness center, a DJ live nightly, an AstroTurf sundeck with private cabanas, and a rooftop poolside bar that stays open way past bedtime. When your batteries finally run down, you can fall into feather bedding. Still, 14-foot-long desks, two-line phones and wireless Internet access reveal an underlying truth here: there's a lot of serious work being done Downtown, even if it's not about oil.

Greater Downtown

Chamberlain

1000 Westmount Dr. (off Holloway Dr.)

Phone:	310-657-7400 or 866-891-0949
Fax:	310-854-6744
Web:	www.chamberlainwesthollywood.com
Prices:	**$$$**

104
Rooms
8
Suites

Kor Hotel Group

Part of the Kor Hotel Group portfolio, this West Hollywood hideaway is a boutique hotel whose 112 guestrooms and suites evoke the ambience of a residential pied-à-terre. The interior design reflects that quality; the décor is personal and intense, far from Minimalist. You'll notice this immediately in the lobby's herringbone-patterned white and green marble floor, mirrored walls, plush seating, jade-green globe lamps, and palette of silver-gray, ice-blue and aqua-green.

Rooms are spacious, each with a small balcony, gas fireplace, and all the music and video equipment you could want. High-thread-count white linens, down pillows and duvet, and a marble bath stocked with fine towels and toiletries sustain a sense of staying with unstinting friends. If work you must, there's an oversized desk and an Internet connection, and a safe large enough to stow your laptop.

Shady cabanas and wood chaise lounges flank the small rectangular rooftop pool, its five-story-high perch affording a panorama of the Hollywood Hills and LA's vast southerly sprawl. There's efficient room service from the Chamberlain Bistro, which serves Californian fare.

Hollywood

Elan

8435 Beverly Blvd. (at Croft Ave.)

Phone: 323-658-6663 or 888-611-0398
Fax: 323-658-6640
Web: www.elanhotel.com
Prices: $$

52
Rooms

Elan

Housed in a striking concrete-and-glass building near Third Street's better restaurants, galleries and shops, this boutique hotel is a great value in this area. The lobby and lounge have avocado-colored walls, with furnishings of tangerine, stone gray, and sea-foam green.

Appointments in the 52 guestrooms are colored from a desert palette of sand, cactus and burnt yellows. The in-room safe accommodates a laptop. Egyptian-cotton linens, down pillows, and a plush robe ensure a high level of comfort, though traffic noise in rooms on the Third Street side of the building can be distracting.

Reasonable garage parking fees, free local phone calls, and free Internet access in the lobby are thoughtful perks. A 25-inch cable television plays videotapes, and the front desk stocks a good film library. Bathrooms are outfitted with plush Irish-cotton towels and high-quality amenities.

You can surf the web while you enjoy a complimentary breakfast of gourmet coffee, fresh fruit and fresh-baked muffins in the Cyber Lounge. There is no pool, but a fitness room includes free weights and exercise machines. Staff members may be small in number, but they are efficient and friendly.

Hollywood

Le Parc

 733 N. West Knoll Dr. (bet. Melrose Ave. & Sherwood Dr.)

Phone: 310-855-8888 or 800-578-4837
Fax: 310-659-7812
Web: www.leparcsuites.com
Prices: $$$

142
Rooms
12
Suites

Le Parc Suite

Hollywood

It's all about comfort at Le Parc. All 154 rooms and suites are classically decorated and range from 650 to 1,000 square feet. Each has a private balcony, a kitchen, a separate sitting area and a fireplace. The largest have separate bedrooms. All have flat-screen TVs; players for CDs, videotapes and DVDs; a mini-bar; a safe; and large closets with bureaus so you can completely settle in. You can bring Fido along, too, for a fee.

You could pound the pavement to work out in this residential neighborhood, but if you prefer to stay on the premises, the hotel has a fitness center and a rooftop pool, a tennis court, a Jacuzzi spa, and a sun deck with views of the Hollywood Hills. Feel like eating in? There's a pleasant restaurant and bar, Knoll, serving Mediterranean-influenced fare from early morning to late night (the bar stays open later). That's Le Parc's pitch, persuasive for those facing a business trip and wanting to add a bit of pleasure to it.

The hotel offers car service within a three-mile radius. That will get you to Beverly Hills, but it's a mile short of the Hollywood Bowl. Knoll, however, will pack a gourmet picnic meal for your evening at the fabled amphitheater.

Sofitel

8555 Beverly Blvd. (at La Cienega Blvd.)

Phone: 310-278-5444
Fax: 310-657-2816
Web: www.sofitel.com
Prices: $$$

295
Rooms

Sofitel Los Angeles

If Beverly Hills shopping is your goal in LA, book a room at the Sofitel. The hotel's location on Beverly Boulevard, across from Beverly Center mall and near the designer boutiques of Rodeo Drive, Robertson Boulevard and Melrose Avenue make it the perfect perch for a sojourn spent exercising your credit card.

Opened in 1989, the Sofitel had a complete facelift in 2006, which renewed the rooms and public spaces with a sleek, contemporary look. Black mirrored columns and ultramodern chairs dot the lobby, while the addition of LeSpa, SIMON LA restaurant *(see restaurant listing)* and the STONE ROSE Lounge—styled in sexy red tones by Cindy Crawford's husband, Rande Gerber—make the Sofitel a place to be seen.

Rooms are done in soft earth tones, with flat-screen TVs, Frette robes, luxurious linens, down duvets, and plush beds; many boast views of the Hollywood Hills. In the bathrooms, thoughtful touches include an oversize rain shower as well as Roger & Gallet bath products. Add a spa, fitness facility, pool and sun deck, plus gracious staff members who go out of their way to see to your comfort, and you're set for a *très confortable* stay.

Hollywood

Sunset Tower

8358 Sunset Blvd. (bet. Olive Dr. & Sweetzer Ave.)

Phone:	323-654-7100 or 800-225-2637
Fax:	323-654-9287
Web:	www.sunsettowerhotel.com
Prices:	$$$$

34 Rooms

40 Suites

Sunset Tower Hotel

Architect Leland Bryant's 15-story apartment house was, from its debut in 1929 as the Argyle, hailed as a splendid marriage of Art Deco and Hollywood style. Scrupulously renovated and maintained, it seems unthinkable that rumors of demolition circulated even after it was added to the National Register of Historic Places in 1980. If its walls could talk, they'd gossip about former residents including Howard Hughes, John Wayne, Marilyn Monroe, Errol Flynn, Elizabeth Taylor, Frank Sinatra and Benjamin Siegel—whom you called "Bugsy" at your peril.

The gangster's 1930s apartment (he was evicted for gambling) is now the lobby and the club-like Tower Bar *(see restaurant listing)*, decorated with brass-inlaid walnut paneling, suede banquettes and a fireplace. From electronics to toiletries, rooms are well-appointed. Floor-to-ceiling windows frame unobstructed views, which by night become a glittering brocade of city lights. The top floors have been reconfigured into penthouse suites with wraparound terraces, and town houses with 20-foot ceilings and stairways to sleeping areas.

The spa, fitness center and pool deck are luxurious, the service quietly efficient.

Hollywood

212

The Ritz-Carlton, Huntington Hotel & Spa

001

1401 S. Oak Knoll Ave. (at Hillcrest Ave)

Phone:	626-568-3900 or 800-241-3333
Fax:	626-585-6420
Web:	www.ritzcarlton.com
Prices:	$$$

366
Rooms

26
Suites

The Ritz-Carlton, Huntington Hotel & Spa

This Mediterranean Revival landmark opened in 1907, setting the Southland standard for grand hotels. A renovation in 1991 raised the bar again, yet the hotel and its 23 acres of lawn and gardens remain anchored in the early-20th-century notion of Southern California as the palmy apotheosis of the American Dream. Debutantes still bow in the ballrooms, and conventioneers still rally over dreams of prosperity like boosters of old.

There's a sense, at this sunny San Marino Valley overlook, of good times past and more to come. Most of the guestrooms are in the eight-story main building. Cottages throughout the grounds account for the rest. All come with featherbeds covered in Egyptian cotton linens, down comforters and pillows; marble baths sumptuously stocked; plush robes; a refreshments cabinet; and a dozen other amenities, including WiFi Internet access. A fully-equipped business center is open 24/7.

The hotel's Dining Room *(see restaurant listing)* serves expertly prepared contemporary fare. For sports fans, a tennis pro presides over three lighted courts, personal trainers staff the fitness center, and two of the four nearby golf courses are championship-rated.

Pasadena

The Ambrose

1255 20th St. (at Arizona Ave.)

Phone:	310-315-1555 or 877-262-7673
Fax:	310-315-1556
Web:	www.ambrosehotel.com
Prices:	$$

77
Rooms

The Ambrose

Santa Monica's handsomest older residences are Craftsman jewels, and this quiet enclave in a residential neighborhood 20 blocks from the beachside bustle blends that style with Asian elements. Earth tones, restrained color accents, and an Asian-inspired garden with a fountain and koi pond reflect the owner's belief in the physical and emotional benefits of applying the Chinese guidelines of feng shui.

That discipline translates into wide, dark-stained wood doors opening into entry areas with wood floors and high ceilings, and the Craftsman signature of dark wood trim. A television hides inside a walnut cabinet; limestone bathrooms use a neutral palette. The effect is an air of tranquility.

Pillows and duvets are down-filled, the linens fine Italian fabric (hypo-allergenic bedding is available on request). There are soft bathrobes, plush towels.

Environmentally conscious policies dictate earth-friendly cleaning compounds, comprehensive recycling, wise energy use, and fair-trade organic coffee served in Urth Caffe. Guests are encouraged to self-park in the underground garage. There's a car-rental facility on-site, with, of course, hybrids for hire.

Casa del Mar

1910 Ocean Way (at Pico Blvd.)

Phone: 310-581-5533 or 800-898-6999
Fax: 310-581-5503
Web: www.hotelcasadelmar.com
Prices: $$$$

112
Rooms

17
Suites

Casa Del Mar

A $65-million facelift ending in 1999 transformed this seven-story brick and sandstone Renaissance Revival edifice into the grand doyenne of local beach hotels. In the common areas, damask and velvet draperies and fruitwood furnishings honor the hotel's vintage (1926). An arched double stairway rises from the entrance foyer to a lofty, paneled lobby of marble floors, wrought-iron light fixtures, and deep-cushioned couches and armchairs suited for tea or cocktails. Floor-to-ceiling windows along the lobby's back wall afford stunning views of the Pacific, as does Catch *(see restaurant listing)*, the hotel's new seafood restaurant.

Guestrooms, spacious and well-appointed, evoke the French Riviera with colorful panache in walls of buttercup yellow framed by white ceilings. Baths of gray Italian marble feature a soaking tub, a separate shower and an abundance of amenities.

The U-shaped building embraces a pool deck opening onto the beach. Skirting the hotel, a bike and walking trail runs 22 miles from Will Rogers State Park (north of Santa Monica) to Torrance Beach near Palos Verdes. On chilly days, the fitness center offers an indoor alternative.

Santa Monica Bay

The Huntley

1111 2nd St. (at California Ave.)

Phone:	310-394-5454
Fax:	310-458-9776
Web:	www.thehuntleyhotel.com
Prices:	$$$

188 Rooms

21 Suites

Jonathan Rouse/The Huntley Hotel

An archetype of contemporary design, The Huntley houses 209 rooms and suites on its 18 floors. Each is bright and airy, most rooms located off softly lit, carpeted hallways. Comfy beds are fitted with crisp white Italian linens and down-filled pillows and duvets. There is a 42-inch plasma TV, a desk big enough for paperwork (with a business center for backup), and a choice of Internet hookups.

Beige travertine marble lines the bathrooms, which are equipped with a spacious glass-enclosed shower and quality bath products. A safe, plush robes for lounging about, and closets large enough to stow luggage complete the in-room amenities.

You can order food 24 hours a day, but why eat in your room when you can dine at The Penthouse *(see restaurant listing)* on contemporary American cuisine in a dazzling setting atop the hotel?

Situated two blocks from the Santa Monica bluffs, the hotel boasts views of rooftops and sea in one direction, and palm-lined city streets and distant mountains in the other. Though there is no pool or outdoor garden, there is a fitness center, and nearby Palisades Park has walking paths, a pretty little rose garden and broad ocean vistas.

Loews Santa Monica Beach

Loews Hotels

1700 Ocean Ave. (bet. Pico Blvd. & Colorado Ave.)

Phone:	310-458-6700 or 800-235-6397
Fax:	310-576-3143
Web:	www.santamonicaloewshotel.com
Prices:	$$$

329 Rooms

13 Suites

Loews really is on the beach, a short stroll from the San Monica Pier's child-friendly amusements, including a historic refurbished carousel. The all-glass atrium lobby affords great beach views.

Guestrooms on the four floors above open onto balconied hallways overlooking the lobby's potted palms and seating areas. Comfortable and spacious, rooms are done in neutral color schemes with accents of gold, beige and taupe. Many have sea views; others glimpse the pool area or Ocean Avenue. A pale gray-green day bed with an overhead lamp for reading adds a sophisticated touch. Thoughtfully appointed baths, divided between the grooming and shower areas, are paneled with creamy handmade tiles flecked with crushed seashells; their opalescent glints lend a subtle sparkle.

Ocean temperatures are chilly, so if you want to swim, stick to the large outdoor lap pool. Extra fees gain you access to the spa and fitness center and the Internet. Room service is efficient, but at the hotel's restaurant, Ocean and Vine, you can enjoy expansive beach views, a firepit filled with glass pebbles, and Californian cuisine mixing various techniques, styles and influences.

Santa Monica Bay

Shutters on the Beach

1 Pico Blvd. (at Appian Way)

Phone:	310-458-0030 or 800-334-9000
Fax:	310-458-4589
Web:	www.shuttersonthebeach.com
Prices:	$$$$

186
Rooms

12
Suites

Shutters

Bright white, like the building's Victorian trim, the shutters here open onto balconies and, in most cases, views of the sand and water. The lobby's peaked ceiling, wood floors and potted palms recall Caribbean clubs, with a fireplace for coolers days. The hotel's twin buildings adjoin her sister, Casa del Mar *(see hotel listing)*, and like her sibling, shelters a pool and sun deck framing a view of the Pacific.

Though not always large, rooms are quite comfortable, sporting a casual-chic white beach motif accented by pale blue, sandy beige and brown. Large wood-framed feather beds are covered with a white duvet and plumped up with feather pillows. Like the rooms' shuttered doors, crown moldings and built-in cabinets for books and electronics are as white as sun-bleached sand. The closet is spacious; the bath boasts a roomy stone shower stall. Fluffy robes and high-quality towels and linens wrap guests in luxury.

Wireless Internet lets you tell friends about your meal at the hotel's restaurant, One Pico *(see restaurant listing)*, and your sightings of celebrity faces gleaming from treatments at One, the hotel's A-list spa.

Santa Monica Bay

218

Viceroy Santa Monica

1819 Ocean Ave. (at Pico Blvd.)

Phone:	310-260-7500 or 866-891-0947
Fax:	310-260-7515
Web:	www.viceroysantamonica.com
Prices:	$$$$

158
Rooms

4
Suites

Kor Hotel Group

A contemporary, cosmopolitan oasis, this celebrity hangout boasts a fine location near the beach. Decked out in Regency style, the common areas, the restaurant, the bar and the spacious guestrooms are painted in shades of gray offset by cream and emerald green.

The white-and-gray theme continues in the guestrooms' pale gray curtains, gray-stained wood entertainment center and gray-marble-topped white nightstands. Emerald silk armchairs add a splash of color. Staying in is a luxurious option when you have a comfy king featherbed with Mascioni linens and oversized down pillows, a large flat-screen TV and a well-stocked mini-bar. In the bathrooms, aromatherapy toiletries add a thoughtful touch.

If you're working, wired and wireless high-speed Internet access is available throughout the property. If you're hungry, Whist *(see restaurant listing)* offers refined Californian cuisine.

The hotel attracts young, affluent club-hoppers whose often-noisy revelry in the bar and restaurant runs to all hours. That's an issue for some, because the rooms are not well sound-proofed. Though the Viceroy is a great place to socialize with the junior A-list, don't count on it for tranquility.

Santa Monica Bay

Four Seasons Westlake Village

 001

2 Dole Dr. (at Via Rocas), Westlake Village

Phone: 818-575-3000 or 800-332-3442
Fax: 818-575-3100
Web: www.fourseasons.com
Prices: $$$

243
Rooms

27
Suites

Barbara Kraft/Four Seasons

The proximity of this opulent 270-room hotel to the California WellBeing Institute creates an unusual opportunity to immerse yourself in a regimen of swimming and exercise, yoga and meditation, spa treatments and healthy dining. There are, however, also the posh tables of Hampton's and Onyx *(see restaurant listing for both)*, and the convivial attitude of The Bar, where the crack of pool balls sets the tone. In other words, balance.

An Asian motif adorns the paneled, marble-floored and flower-decorated lobby, which would put a Swiss banker at ease. A corps of well-trained concierges, receptionists and valets stands at the ready.

Decorated with English Regency furniture and primary colors of blue and gold, rooms feature Italian-inspired fabrics and include a spacious desk and office chairs, a cushy armchair with footrest, and a plasma TV. Large floor-to-ceiling windows let in ample light. The feather bed is large, and the beige marble bathroom has a big soaking tub and a separate glass-enclosed stone shower stall.

A glass-roofed atrium building shelters an indoor pool. It adjoins the outdoor patio where you can lounge to the soothing rush of a waterfall.

Ventura Boulevard

Hyatt Regency Century Plaza

2025 Avenue of the Stars (bet Constellation & Olympic Blvds.)

Phone:	310-228-1234 or 800-233-1234
Fax:	310-551-7548
Web:	www.centuryplaza.hyatt.com
Prices:	$$$

680 Rooms

46 Suites

Hyatt Hotels & Resorts

Where cowboys wearing makeup once shot it out on dusty streets, business people now do battle in meeting rooms, most unaware that this recently remodeled 19-story hotel stands on what was once the back lot of the 20th Century Fox studio. The master plan for Century City, unveiled in 1957 as a "second" downtown, included architect Minoru Yamasaki's centerpiece, shaped like a parenthesis and facing a boulevard of fountains.

Recline by its big square pool and your view is of high-rise towers. No wonder business is on the minds of most guests, or that the hotel serves their need for places to meet, entertain, rally the troops and work off stress. Accordingly, a multilingual staff operates a full-service business center, and the house restaurant Breeze *(see restaurant listing)* serves superb Californian fare.

Spacious guestrooms follow the hotel's motif of dark browns, beige and black. Furnishings include a large black-marble-topped desk and slate-gray armchairs. Comfortable down beds are covered with quality cotton linens; bathrooms have wood paneling and marble floors. Enjoy panoramic sunrise or sunset views from your private balcony.

Westside

W - Westwood

002

930 Hilgard Ave. (at Le Conte Ave.)

Phone: 310-208-8765
Fax: 310-824-0355
Web: www.whotels.com
Prices: $$$$

258
Suites

W Hotels

The W's 15 ivy-covered concrete stories dominate a residential street near UCLA, but plantation shutters, dense foliage, and a discreet entrance betrayed only by the valet-parking shuffle below camouflage the trendy world within.

One clue is the water running beneath the front steps to glass doors opening into the lobby, where low, cushioned benches and tables declare a devotion to modernity. Look left and you'll see the Whiskey Blue bar and the restaurant Nine-Thirty, serving an American menu featuring local produce, artisan cheeses and boutique wines. Another clue is the names given to the W's one- and two-room suites, which range from 400 to 1,400 square feet. The smallest are billed as Wonderful, Spectacular and Fabulous. Then come the Mega, the Wow, and the Extreme Wow. All have beds with goose-down pillows and comforters, fancy linens, cushy sofas, oversize work desks and high-speed Internet access (for a fee), plus the full array of video and audio equipment.

With its small pool ringed by lounge chairs and cabana tents, the Backyard is a scene. The palpable ambition of the mostly young, up-and-coming crowd here adds a very LA frisson to the air.

Notes

Notes

Notes

Notes

Notes

Notes

Notes

Notes

Notes

Notes

Notes

Notes

Notes

Notes

Notes

Notes

Notes

Notes